dopting in Massachusetts

Center For Adoption Research
University of Massachusetts

William M. Bulger, President
University of Massachusetts

Aaron Lazare, M.D., Chancellor
University of Massachusetts Worcester
Executive Director, Center for Adoption Research

Peter Gibbs, M.A.
Director

Jack Demick, Ph.D.
Research Director

Diane Zapach
Associate Director

Adopting in Massachusetts

Introduction 5
Adopting in Massachusetts
Center for Adoption Research
Acknowledgement
Considering Adoption
Three Types of Adoption

Choosing an Approach 15

1
Basic Steps in Adoption
Exploring Your Options
Adoption and Diversity
Choosing an Approach
Selecting an Agency
Application Process
Homestudy
Waiting
Match and Placement
Post-Placement Period
Finalization

Domestic Infant Adoption 29

Overview
Agency-Identified Adoption
Parent-Identified and Agency-Assisted Adoption
Information About the Child
Interstate Adoption
Surrender or Termination of Parental Rights
The Role of Attorneys
Birthparent Allowable Expenses
A Word About Birthparents
Openness in Adoption

International Adoption 39

Overview
Two Basic Approaches
Health Concerns
Application Process
Immigration and Naturalization Service
Matching in International Adoption
Information About the Child
Processing the Adoption
Adjusting to a New World
International Adoption Documentation Checklist

Adopting a Waiting-Child 49

4
Overview
Placement of Siblings
Application
MAPP Training and Homestudy
The Match Process
Placement Planning
Post-Placement Process

Fees, Adoption Subsidy and the Adoption Tax Credit 57

5
Overview
Component Fees
Cost of Adopting
Costs in Waiting-Child Adoption
Financial Assistance
Adoption Subsidy
Adoption Tax Credit

After You Adopt 63

6
Finalization is a Beginning
Growing Up with Adoption
Many Kinds of Adoption
Post-Adoption Support and Services

Resource Guide 69

7
Support and Informational Resources
Bibliography
Adoption Agencies

Credits

Senior Editor
Peter Gibbs

Assistant Editor
Lisa Kirby

Contributing Editor
Barbara Perry

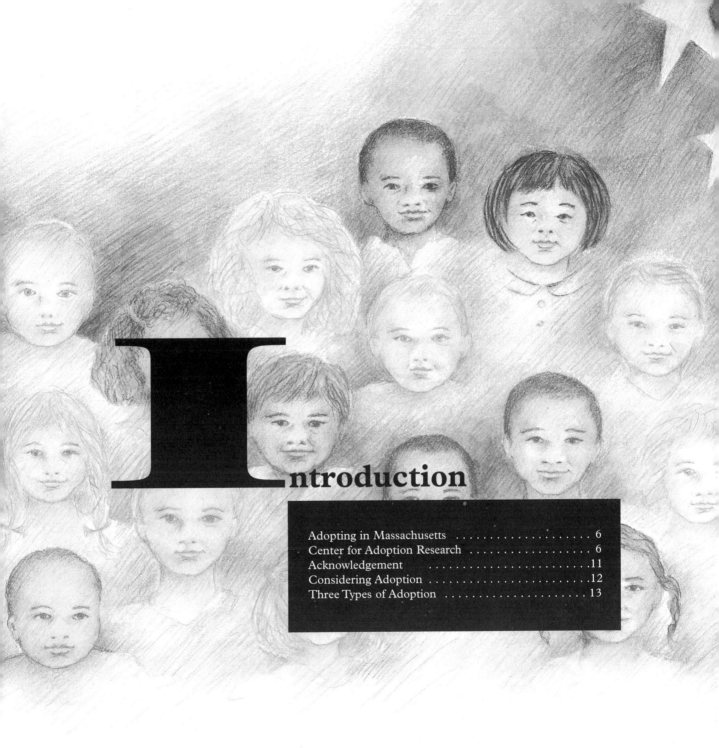

Introduction

Adopting in Massachusetts 6
Center for Adoption Research 6
Acknowledgement 11
Considering Adoption 12
Three Types of Adoption 13

Adopting in Massachusetts

This guide was produced with the generous support of Helene R. Cahners-Kaplan and Carol R. Goldberg, Trustees, The Sidney and Esther Rabb Charitable Foundations and Paul D. Boudreau, Esquire and Elizabeth D. Scheibel, Esquire. Special appreciation is also extended to Deborah Rabb Goldberg and Michael A. Gaffin, Esquire, for their assistance with this project.

The Center for Adoption Research at the University of Massachusetts developed this first edition of *Adopting in Massachusetts* as an informational guide to help people who are beginning to think about adoption as a way to create or add to a family. It is also intended to support professionals in the field who assist couples and individuals in completing the adoption process.

Adopting a child is a wonderful, intensely emotional and unforgettable experience. It is also a complicated process with many steps. Sorting out the procedural details, while managing a wide array of emotions, can make the adoption process challenging. This book will provide you with comprehensive information about the different kinds of adoption and guide you through the steps in the adoption process. We have condensed key information about the options available, to help you make informed decisions so you can be confident in your choices. We wish you well on your journey toward adopting.

Center For Adoption Research

... providing practical responses to real world issues raised by foster care and adoption.

The Center for Adoption Research is a five-campus initiative of the University of Massachusetts, based at the UMass Medical School in Worcester. It is the first university-based Center in the nation, with the sole purpose of providing practical responses to real world issues raised by foster care and adoption.

The mission of the Center is to conduct research, analyze and develop policy, and promote educational and training programs on foster care and adoption to ensure that every child can be raised in a permanent loving home.

The Center is supported by charitable donations made by individuals, corporations and foundations. All contributions are tax-deductible to the extent of the law. If you would like to make a contribution to the Center please call us at 508-856-5397, or use the response card at the back of this guidebook.

THE COMMONWEALTH OF MASSACHUSETTS
EXECUTIVE DEPARTMENT
STATE HOUSE • BOSTON 02133
(617) 727-3600

ARGEO PAUL CELLUCCI
GOVERNOR

JANE SWIFT
LIEUTENANT GOVERNOR

Dear Friends:

      The Cellucci-Swift Administration remains committed to ensuring that each child has a safe, nurturing and permanent home. Through our Assignment Adoption initiative, we have doubled the number of children adopted in Massachusetts over the last few years. Lieutenant Governor Jane Swift and I are proud of that accomplishment, and we sincerely appreciate the help and support of our many partners in the religious, business, academic and civic communities involved in this endeavor.

      Indeed, we are fortunate to have the Center for Adoption Research & Policy at the University of Massachusetts as one of our partners. *Adopting in Massachusetts* is a guide for prospective parents which the Center has prepared and distributed throughout the Commonwealth as a public service.

      Each and every day, children come into the care of the Commonwealth, and some of these children need an adoptive family. Currently, there are just under 1,000 children waiting for a permanent home with an adoptive family. Despite the high level of interest in adoption throughout the Commonwealth, a number of prospective adoptive parents have been turned away due to the lack of easily accessible and reliable information about the adoption process.

      We need every family who is interested in adopting to pursue that interest. *Adopting in Massachusetts* is a consumer-friendly guide. My hope is that this guide will help connect families who want to adopt with our children who are waiting.

      My thanks to the University of Massachusetts Center for Adoption Research & Policy for developing *Adopting in Massachusetts*, and my thanks and encouragement to each prospective adoptive parent who reads this guide.

             Sincerely,

             Argeo Paul Cellucci

THE COMMONWEALTH OF MASSACHUSETTS
OFFICE OF THE ATTORNEY GENERAL
ONE ASHBURTON PLACE
BOSTON. MASSACHUSETTS 02108-1698

THOMAS F. REILLY
ATTORNEY GENERAL

(617) 727-2200

Dear Prospective Adoptive Parent:

One of the most socially useful and personally rewarding endeavors a caring and responsible adult can undertake is to serve as the adoptive parent for a child who, for whatever reason, cannot remain in his or her home of origin. I am delighted that your interest in adoption has led you to pick up and peruse this enormously useful book.

Members of the Office of the Attorney General, in concert with others both inside and outside of state government, have worked tirelessly in recent years to reform and streamline the adoption process in Massachusetts, to help rewrite the rules of court that govern adoption and child welfare proceedings, and to help develop new "permanency" options for children in need of substitute care. Adopting in Massachusetts is an important complement to these efforts to improve the adoption process in our state.

You, and others like you, who are willing to make a commitment to love and nurture a child not linked to you biologically are without question *the* linchpin -- and *the* indispensable ingredient -- in an effective adoption system in this state. Not only do you deserve our immense gratitude and support, but now, thanks to the University of Massachusetts Center for Adoption Research and Policy, you can benefit from all of the comprehensive, practical information and advice about adoption contained in this guide. I commend you for your public-spiritedness and urge you to take full advantage of this valuable book.

Sincerely,

Tom Reilly

OFFICE OF THE PRESIDENT

MASSACHUSETTS SENATE

STATE HOUSE, BOSTON 02133-1007

THOMAS F. BIRMINGHAM
PRESIDENT

ROOM 332
TEL. (617) 722-1500

Dear Friend:

The booklet you hold in your hands is the first comprehensive and practical guide for prospective adoptive parents in the Commonwealth. In creating *Adopting in Massachusetts*, the Center for Adoption Research and Policy at the University of Massachusetts has lit a path through a murky and often intimidating process.

There are two worlds of adoption in Massachusetts today. The first belongs to public adoption, where more than 3,000 of the approximately 12,000 children in foster care await permanent homes. There are not enough adoptive families for those children. Yet the second world of private infant adoption sees four or five couples or individuals seeking to adopt for each child placed with an agency.

This tragic paradox mirrors national trends—a rising number of children entering the foster care system and ultimately needing adoptive families, as well as increasing numbers of couples and individuals seeking to adopt. The Department of Health and Human Services estimates that as many as 700,000 children will spend part of the year in foster care nationwide.

Although there is a high level of interest in adoption throughout the Commonwealth, a lack of accessible, reliable information about the process has turned many away. This guide includes explanations of procedures for the public system, private agencies, and international options. It also outlines important legal, financial, and health issues of concern to anyone contemplating adoption.

It is my hope that this guide will help end the anxious wait of children and adults who want a family. Few actions have the power to transform lives and heal wounds like a successful adoption.

I thank the University of Massachusetts for this exemplary effort to fulfill its public service mission by creating and distributing *Adopting in Massachusetts* at no charge. It is an invaluable resource for those of our neighbors who seek to build new and healthy families.

Very Truly Yours,

Thomas F. Birmingham

The Commonwealth of Massachusetts

House of Representatives

State House, Boston 02133-1008

THOMAS M. FINNERAN
SPEAKER

———

ROOM 356
OFFICE PHONE
722-2500

Dear Prospective Parent:

There is no greater gift than the life-altering and elevating act of adopting a child. It is a singularly unique gift – a gift where you not only give but also receive. Adoptive parents provide children with a safe and nurturing home, and they give them renewed life, lasting hope, and a brighter future. Quite simply, our world becomes a better place in which to live when the home of just one good person becomes the home of an adopted child.

On behalf of so many children in need of a family, I thank you for even the simple act of reading this guide. By doing so, you may have already begun to change and influence the course of a child's life. It is my sincere hope that the guide will answer the many questions and allay the various concerns which accompany the adoption of a child. Those concerns are not a surprise. Indeed, most adoptive parents raised the very same questions when they first gave thought to sharing their lives. The joys and successes of those adoptive parents are a testament to their generous spirits and to the notion that there is always room for love and commitment in our lives.

In 1998, I invited my colleagues in the Legislature to join me in an effort to make comprehensive changes to our adoption system. In 1999, we improved the way the government helps adoptive children move through the legal system into the loving homes and shared lives of adoptive parents. The law is now far more friendly to pre-adoptive parents and to the children they hope to welcome home. Please be assured that should you choose to adopt, the Commonwealth of Massachusetts and its licensed agencies will support you each step of the way.

The pages which follow are designed to provide you guidance and information about the process. The inspiration to follow through that process is obviously in your heart. I hope that you will act on that inspiration.

Sincerely yours,

THOMAS M. FINNERAN
Speaker of the House

Acknowledgment

This guide would not have been possible without the dedication and good work of private and public agencies, professionals, advocates, legislators and jurists who have contributed to the policies and practices in adoption. We would like to thank the Governor, the Attorney General, the Senate President and the Speaker of the House for their commitment to families whose lives are touched by foster care and adoption. We would like to thank Mary Gambon, Leo Farley, Donna Hollis, Kelly Barnhart and the supervisors and workers of the Department of Social Services, who provided important information and perspective.

Special thanks to Dr. Ruth McRoy, Director, Center for Social Work Research, Ruby Lee Piester Centennial Professor in Services to Children and Families, from the University of Texas at Austin School of Social Work for her thoughtful suggestions regarding adoption and diversity.

Since adoptive families are the real experts and guides in the lifelong experience of adoption, we would also like to thank Howard Fain, Leslie Linson, Kitty Ford and Jerry Daly, Debra Olshever and Monica and Sam Guckenheimer for sharing the wisdom gained from their experiences. Their feedback and suggestions have been invaluable in developing this guide.

Finally, we would like to extend our appreciation to Margie Mintz, illustrator, author and adoptive mother, for creating our cover design with understanding and sensitivity.

Considering Adoption

People come to consider adoption for a variety of reasons. Many, who would like to create or add to a family, turn to adoption when they find that, due to infertility, they are not able to have a child by birth. If you are experiencing infertility, a few things are important to think about when deciding whether or not adoption is right for you. For instance, how do you feel about your infertility? It is normal to have a wide range of feelings, such as shame, despair, inferiority and anger. If you often find yourself angry and preoccupied by the unfairness of it all, you may need more time before you are ready to adopt. Some people feel a strong desire to have a child that resembles them, or a need to carry on their genes. Adoption may not be the right choice in this case. If after self-reflection you conclude that being a parent is more important than how you become a parent, then you should actively explore the possibility of adopting.

Some people choose to adopt for reasons other than infertility. Many people believe that if they have the capacity, they should offer their home to a child who needs one. They may already have children or have raised children to adulthood. Others may choose to provide a home for a child in need rather than bring a new child into the world. Some people have genetic conditions they don't want to pass on, or a medical condition that makes the risks associated with giving birth very high.

In thinking about whether adoption is right for you, it is important to consider how your extended family might react to having a child join the family through adoption. Would they be welcoming or apprehensive? What, if anything, might you need to talk about with your family to have the support you need to adopt?

Many issues arise when considering adoption as a way to create or add to a family. Often when people first begin to think about adoption, it just doesn't seem right. For couples, it is normal for each partner to feel differently about the idea of adopting, especially at the beginning of the process. Over time, as people do more exploring and learning, they become more comfortable with the idea of being adoptive parents. Adoption isn't right for everybody and, for some, there may be a long, winding path to travel before deciding that it is the right choice for them.

Three Types of Adoption

In Massachusetts there are three basic types of adoption:

Kind of Adoption	Children	Typical time to complete
Domestic	Newborns & Infants	12-36 months
International	3-24 months and older, up to age 16	9-24 months
Waiting Child from public foster care	Some 0-5 years of age, many children over the age of 6	12-60 months

Some agencies offer more than one approach to adoption. The following chapter provides an overview of the basic steps involved in adopting. Don't worry if the terms for the approaches to adoption are unfamiliar. Additional sections of the guide will provide detailed information for each approach. By the time you finish reading, you'll know how to move toward the adoption that is right for you or where to go for additional guidance.

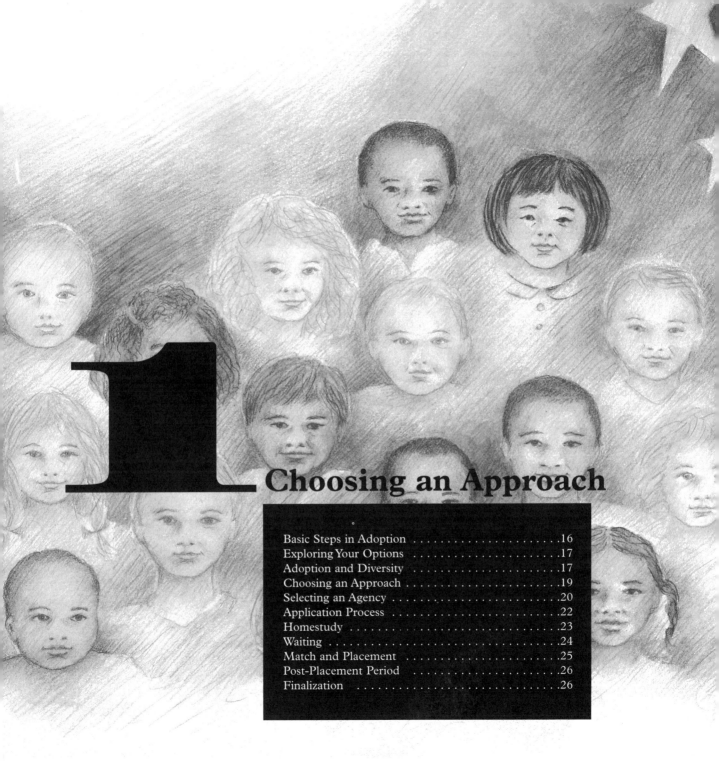

1 Choosing an Approach

Basic Steps in Adoption 16
Exploring Your Options 17
Adoption and Diversity 17
Choosing an Approach 19
Selecting an Agency 20
Application Process 22
Homestudy 23
Waiting 24
Match and Placement 25
Post-Placement Period 26
Finalization 26

Basic Steps in Adoption

Finalization

Post-Placement

Placement

Placement Planning

Matching

The Wait

The Homestudy

The Application

Selecting an Agency

Choosing Your Approach

Exploring Your Options

Exploring Your Options

Whether you are just considering adoption or are ready to begin the process, you will need to decide which type of adoption best "fits" with you and your family. You can begin exploring this by reading books and articles on adoption (see Bibliography on page 74) and talking to adoptive families and professionals.

Two excellent resources to use early in the process are the Open Door Society (ODS) and Resolve of the Bay State (see Resource Guide on page 71 for contact information). Both organizations offer information sessions about adoption and connections with people who can share their experiences with you. It is also helpful to contact adoption agencies, which usually have staff members available to answer questions and provide an overview of their programs. Most agencies also offer information packets that include descriptions of their programs, orientation procedures, any requirements, and the evaluation and approval processes.

Anyone who wants to adopt in Massachusetts needs to understand that only agencies licensed through the Office of Child Care Services (OCCS) or the Department of Social Services (DSS) are allowed to place children for adoption. DSS is the public agency whose adoption placement services focus primarily on waiting children in foster care who are in need of permanent loving families. There are also more than 36 private, licensed agencies in Massachusetts that provide adoption placement services (see Resource Guide on page 77). These agencies may provide infant adoption, international adoption and, in coordination with DSS, waiting-child adoption placement services.

Adoption and Diversity

Among the many kinds of adoption are those in which parents and children are from different ethnic and racial heritages.

American society has become more diverse in the last 25 years. There are more different kinds of families than ever before. There are two-parent and single-parent families, divorced families, step-parent and blended families, interracial families, international families, gay and lesbian families, grandparents parenting grandchildren, families formed through surrogacy and families formed through a variety of assisted reproductive technologies. This variety makes it easier for adoptive parents to help their children understand that adoption is simply one of the many normal ways in which families are formed in America. It also helps adults, like teachers and physicians, who may play important roles in the lives of adopted children, be more understanding. Adoptive families benefit from this diversity, yet they still must address the impact of adoption on their lives.

Among the many kinds of adoption are those in which parents and children are from different ethnic and racial heritages. These adoptions may be called transcultural or transracial adoptions, but it takes more than two words to encompass the experience. Some people describe these adoptions as interracial, biracial, multicultural and multiracial. In many families, children and parents do not look alike, but for families in which children and parents look ethnically or racially different, the fact of adoption is often more apparent to outsiders. These families often report that strangers, professionals and even friends and relatives can make insensitive and intrusive comments that can be very hurtful. These comments can be hurtful to the child as well as to the parent. Parents are more likely to have to address issues related to adoption with their children and others at unexpected times. Parents often must deal with issues of racism and intolerance that are entirely unfamiliar to them from their own developmental experience. They need to consider the impact on children as they encounter racism, intolerance and ignorance from peers and adults. Oftentimes, parents are completely unaware of racist remarks directed at their children.

Parents often must deal with issues of racism and intolerance that are entirely unfamiliar to them from their own developmental experience.

Transcultural and transracial adoptions bring different experiences to families. Adopting a child of African-American heritage is different from adopting a transcultural child from China or other countries due to negative stereotypes often associated with African-American individuals in our society. Transracial children and families tend to have more to address with peers, friends, strangers, teachers and other professionals. Racial prejudice poses significant challenges to children and families. Children must acknowledge their ethnic and racial identities and deal with negative stereotypes in addition to dealing with their adoptive identity. Children may not raise such concerns with their parents. It is important for parents to take the initiative and be pro-active in dealing with these issues.

Transracial and transcultural adoptions can be very successful. People who consider these approaches to adoption need to know that adopting transculturally or transracially makes a family a multiracial or multiethnic family. Parents must assess their own values and attitudes. They should realistically evaluate the resources and limitations of their social support systems (i.e. family and friends), their community and schools. One of the most important questions is not whether parents can find ways to support their child's connection to his or her cultural heritage, but how can parents themselves truly participate in that culture? How can they make it part of daily family life? How can they be committed to confronting whatever challenges may come related to race and ethnicity? Parents need to understand important contemporary as well as historical aspects of racism. Parents should have, or seek to establish, relationships with adults of the same background as the child. Through these relationships, they may come to understand the issues children may experience and be prepared to help them deal with the social realities of our society. These relationships may also provide role model opportunities down the road. Additionally, parents will need to develop skills to advocate for their children.

Parents should explore the issues involved in transracial and multiracial adoption as they consider whether these approaches to adopting are right for them. Families who have completed transracial or multicultural adoptions are excellent resources for information and support.

Adoption agencies can connect you with families; you can meet them through adoptive family support organizations or even through internet adoption sites. Agencies and support organizations can also assist you in identifying professionals who will help you learn about these kinds of adoptive experiences. In addition, there are books and articles on transracial and multicultural adoption that can be found in book stores, libraries and on the internet. Use the resource guide at the back of this book to identify informational and support resources.

Families who have completed transracial or multicultural adoptions are excellent resources for information and support.

Choosing an Approach

Three Types of Adoption

Domestic Infant

International

Waiting Child

Before deciding which approach to adoption is right for you, think about the characteristics of a child that you would feel comfortable adopting. Most people have an image of their child in mind. Start with this. You also will need to consider how a child would fit into your extended family, your neighborhood and schools. Many people find it helpful to talk to people who have adopted in a variety of ways and to consult with professionals who are knowledgeable about adoption. Learning as much as you can from adoptive families and professionals and clarifying your own desires and needs will help you decide which approach to adoption is best for you.

CHARACTERISTICS OF CHILDREN THAT VARY

- age
- race and ethnic background
- country of origin
- physical, educational, emotional and adjustment needs
- sibling relationships

CHARACTERISTICS OF THE PROCESS THAT VARY

- the costs
- the length of time from the initial application to finalization
- typical relationships or contact with birthparent(s) during and after the adoption
- travel requirements (particularly, though not limited to, international adoptions)

Selecting an Agency

Agency orientations afford prospective adoptive parents the opportunity to meet agency staff and listen to other pre-adoptive parents.

Once you have chosen the approach or approaches to adoption that interest you, attend agency information (or orientation) sessions to learn more about the process and narrow down your options. You should be looking for an agency with a style and philosophy that suits you. Through orientation sessions you can learn about the agency, its programs and services, the children served by the agency, legal requirements, the rights and responsibilities of adoptive parents, matching procedures and the timeline for completing an adoption. Most important, orientations afford prospective adoptive parents the opportunity to meet agency staff and to listen to other pre-adoptive parents.

Sometimes people feel inhibited about asking questions or raising issues at an orientation or information session. They don't want to be seen as not knowing enough, as insensitive or maybe even difficult. You can be sure, however, that any question or concern you have is also on the minds of many other prospective adoptive parents. In fact, many problems and misunderstandings can be avoided by addressing concerns or questions as they arise. It's not easy to feel empowered and be pro-active throughout the process, but the agency orientations are a good place to start being assertive.

The following are some questions to consider asking at agency orientations:

GENERAL QUESTIONS

❏ How many children were placed in the last two years for specific programs?

❏ Are there any restrictions that apply to applicants?

❏ What is the typical total cost for adopting? What services are included in the fixed fees? What fees are variable? What has been the highest total cost? Is there a sliding fee scale for services based on income?

❏ Is there a wait to begin a homestudy?

❏ What is the average time to wait for placement?

❏ What types of educational programs are offered for pre-adoptive and adoptive families?

❏ How does the matching process work?

❏ What kind of information does the agency provide regarding the health, development and history of children and birth parents? When do they provide this?

❏ Can applicants talk with other families who have used the agency's services?

❏ What happens if you turn down a match/placement opportunity?

❏ What pre- and post-placement support services are available?

❏ What kind of prenatal and early infancy information is available?

QUESTIONS FOR INFANT ADOPTION

❏ Are most infants born in Massachusetts or out of state?

❏ Do the birthparents usually choose the adoptive parents?

❏ What is the process for selecting and referring adoptive parents to the birthparents for a potential match?

❏ Do parents usually meet the birthparents?

❏ What resources does the agency use to locate birthparents in need of services?

❏ In what percentage of adoptions do the birthfathers participate by signing a voluntary surrender of parental rights?

QUESTIONS FOR INTERNATIONAL ADOPTION

❏ With what countries does the agency work?

❏ Does the agency network with other programs throughout the country to locate placement resources?

❏ What is the average wait for referral of a child, from different countries, after completion of the homestudy?

❏ Does the agency provide education and support resources regarding the cultural issues involved in international adoption?

❏ How does the agency work with the different governmental systems like INS to expedite adoption applications?

❏ What happens if a particular country's adoption program closes due to political or economic crises?

QUESTIONS FOR WAITING CHILD ADOPTIONS

❑ What kind of information is provided to help you decide if you are a good fit for a particular child?

❑ How are pre-placement meetings and visits with the child, foster parents and birthparents conducted?

❑ What role might the birthparents play in an adoption?

❑ What post-placement services and resources to address specific concerns are offered by the agency?

WHEN CONSIDERING A PARTICULAR CHILD

❑ Why did the child come into foster care?

❑ How many placements has the child had? If more than one, why was the child moved?

❑ What are the child's strengths and vulnerabilities? What kind of attachment behavior has the child exhibited? Who is the child most attached to? What adjustment problems have been observed that relate to prior placement?

❑ What are the details of the child's medical and psychological history? What information is available about the prenatal and early infancy period?

❑ Is this child "legally free" for adoption or is he/she a "legal risk" placement?

Application Process

The application provides the agency with:

• initial information about you

• some of the necessary documents and information needed to meet Massachusetts' regulations and begin a homestudy.

Once you choose an agency, you will be asked to complete an application. In some cases, the application process may include a "pre-application." Agencies may charge a fee when an application is submitted. In Massachusetts, application fees range from $0-$1,000. There are no fees for waiting-child adoptions through the Department of Social Services (DSS) adoption program. Many private agencies waive or reduce fees for people who adopt a waiting child.

The application package requires general identifying information such as date and place of birth, dates of marriages and divorces, education and work histories, financial history and description of residence. Additional documents include birth certificates, marriage certificates and/or divorce decrees, tax returns, a written statement from a physician regarding the health of each member of the household, written references and a Criminal Offender Record Information (CORI).

While you may feel overwhelmed by the amount of information required, these materials are necessary to help the agency get to know you, and most are required by Massachusetts regulation. After the application package has been completed, you will be called, usually within 30 days, to schedule a homestudy.

Homestudy

A homestudy is an assessment required for all adoptions completed in Massachusetts. The fee for homestudies ranges from $850-$3,400 (in many cases there is no fee for waiting-child adoptions). In the best situations it can be an inspiring and educational process, but it can also cause anxiety and stress, as prospective parents worry about being judged by agency professionals. It is important to remember that agencies are not looking for super humans. In general, they are looking for honest, caring people, who show openness to the differences inherent to adoption as well as a willingness to learn. Being real about who you are and forthright about your questions and concerns is helpful in this process.

There are three aspects of the homestudy process. The first, mandated by the state, is to assess your basic fitness and to assure that you can provide a safe and secure environment for a child. Agencies are required to provide you with their criteria for this assessment. The second prepares you for the issues that may arise in the adoption process, as well as in the lifelong experience of being an adoptive family. The third allows the agency to get to know and understand who you are and what type of family you hope to have. This is important for creating a successful matching process with either a birthparent considering an adoption plan in infant adoption, a child in foster care in waiting-child adoption or a referral of a child through a foreign authority in international adoption. Parent education programs may be offered or required along with the homestudy meetings.

The homestudy frequently involves at least four meetings with an assigned adoption professional, at least one of which will be in your home. For married couples, the homestudy also includes meetings with each individual. If additional family members or others (children or relatives, friends, etc.) live in your home they will also meet in an appropriate manner with the adoption worker. This may be an individual meeting or a meeting in which you participate.

While homestudy discussions vary, some basic issues are always covered. These include questions about your background, your upbringing and your relationship with your parents and siblings. Couples will be asked about how they met, how they resolve differences and future parenting roles. Other adoption issues include your motivation for adopting, views toward acceptance of an adopted child, child rearing and discipline, attitudes toward birthparents, and the incorporation of adoption into the lifelong parenting process. The homestudy also presents an opportunity for you to talk through the characteristics of the child you would consider adopting including age, race and ethnicity, birthparent and child social and medical histories, possible medical conditions and developmental disabilities.

The homestudy is completed with a written report prepared by the adoption counselor.

Should the agency have concerns during the homestudy, it will address them during the process. Approval of the homestudy cannot be made until at least 30 days have elapsed since the initial formal contact with the agency. Applicants are notified of the homestudy results within one month of their last session. Once you have an approved homestudy, you are eligible to adopt and the wait begins.

Waiting

There are many ways to cope with the uncertainties and emotional stress of the waiting process.

Waiting for a match at times can be difficult. People describe feeling as if their life has been "put on hold" or are frustrated because they have no control over a process that is so important in their lives. There are numerous ways to cope with the uncertainties and the emotional stress of the waiting process. One way is to stay connected with your agency. Discuss with your adoption worker how often you should check in. Also, many agencies provide education and support groups for waiting parents. The frequency of these groups may vary; many will run monthly or weekly meetings for a determined period of time. Some are ongoing and provide support during the waiting period. Adoptive parents often find that one of the most useful components of these sessions is the ability to meet other pre-adoptive parents who are experiencing many of the same questions, concerns, joys and stresses. Many adoptive parent group discussions include such topics as loss and grief in infertility and adoption, talking with extended family and birthparents, managing the wait, preparing for the placement and issues that will arise in raising an adopted child. You can also take advantage and fill this time by reading books on parenting and adoption, attending adoption- and parenting-related seminars and joining support groups.

Take good care of yourself, physically and emotionally during the waiting period. Improve your diet or start exercising to get in shape for parenting. If this is your first child, start thinking of yourself as an expectant mother or father. Start thinking about what you might put in the nursery or older child's room. In other words, start believing it will really happen. Adoption works. It's just the how and the when that are not always clear. Also, it helps to decide how you will handle questions from friends and relatives. Often, prospective parents feel as if they are constantly asked, "have you heard anything?" during the waiting period. You may want to tell friends and relatives not to ask you about the process, assuring them you'll share news when you're ready.

Match and Placement

In adoption, the first connection between pre-adoptive parents and a child or birthparent(s) is called the "match." It happens differently depending on the approach to adoption you choose, and even has a different name in international adoption — "referral." Regardless of the kind of adoption there are some common themes to this experience. For example, at the time of the match or referral, you are given basic information that may include the race and national origin of the child, and birthfamily and background information about the history, psychological and medical status of the birthparents. If the child is not yet born, as is common in domestic-infant adoption, basic prenatal information will be provided. For older children, more information will be given regarding history, current care, health and well-being.

If you accept the match or referral, the process moves forward. Plans should be made to give you more detailed information regarding medical history, mental health history, and a summary of the child's legal status, as well as any other information relevant to the child's growth and development.

One difficult aspect of adoption is that the kind and amount of information available to parents is often limited.

One difficult aspect of adoption is that there are often limitations on the kind and amount of information available to parents. This can be frustrating and even frightening at times. Each adopting parent or couple must decide what information they must have to agree to the placement of a particular child. Remember that you don't have to say yes to a match. It is normal to feel pressure when presented with a matching situation. Just remind yourself that your needs and questions are important; at the same time, it is also important to be flexible.

When significant medical or psychological risks are involved, parents must make hard decisions. It is always advisable to get competent professional advice and to discuss your concerns with your agency's personnel.

In some situations, there may be specific concerns regarding the health of the child or unresolved questions about the birthfamily's medical and psychological history at the time of the placement. In these situations, the agency will likely ask you to sign a statement acknowledging that you are accepting the placement with the understanding that there may be certain medical or psychological risks. Even when no specific health risks are known, many agencies ask parents to sign a statement acknowledging that the agency cannot be responsible for the future physical or mental health of a child being placed.

Once there is an agreement about the match, the agency develops specific plans to determine where and how placement will take place. Since the details of placement in infant, waiting-child and international adoption differ, refer to the specific sections in the guide for more information. Keep in mind that in adoption, it is normal for plans to change. It doesn't mean that things are not working out, although it may feel that way. A wise person once said that no matter what you think your adoption will look like, it won't. Your adoption will be unique and will probably require you to be flexible when you are feeling very vulnerable.

Adoption agencies usually charge an adoption placement fee when a child is placed. Placement fees in Massachusetts range from $1,000-$29,000 depending on the approach to adoption and the particular circumstances.*

Post-Placement Period

During the post-placement period, adoptive families have monthly contact with an adoption professional.

In Massachusetts, six months must pass from the date of placement before parents may petition legally to finalize an adoption. This is called the "post-placement period." During this time, adoptive families have monthly contacts with an adoption professional from the placement or supervising agency. The contacts focus on family adjustment and the health and development of the child. At least two of these contacts involve meetings in the adoptive parents' home; others are a combination of telephone conversations and meetings that may take place at the agency. Contacts continue until the finalization of the adoption.

Adoptive parents often find that these meetings provide support as well as ideas for adjusting to the new family arrangement, working through language barriers, answering questions, and exploring adoption issues in general.

The fees charged for post-placement services (usually both the post-placement meetings and preparation of the agency documents for the finalization) range from $700-$2,200.*

Finalization

Remember to bring a camera. Finalization photos are a great contribution to the family album.

The finalization is the court event in which adoptive parents become the legal parents of their adopted child. As you might imagine, this is a memorable, emotional experience. Remember to bring a camera. Finalization photos are a great contribution to the family album. The finalization occurs in the probate and family courts in the county in which the parents reside. The agency files a petition for adoption, usually through its attorney, and the court sets a date for the adoptive parents to appear for the finalization. The signing of the adoption decree is the highlight of a judge's day. Many judges will help families create meaningful rituals in this experience. Legal fees associated with the finalization process typically range from $220-$1,500.*

There are no fees for waiting-child adoptions through the Department of Social Services (DSS) adoption program. Many private agencies waive or reduce fees for people who adopt a waiting child.

Notes

2

Domestic Infant Adoption

Overview 30
Agency-Identified Adoption 30
Parent-Identified
and Agency-Assisted Adoption 31
Information About the Child 32
Interstate Adoption 32
Surrender or Termination
of Parental Rights 32
The Role of Attorneys 34
Birthparent Allowable Expenses 35
A Word About Birthparents 35
Openness in Adoption 36

Overview

Differences in approaches to domestic adoption relate primarily to the roles that adoptive parents and the agency play in identifying birthparent(s) who are considering making an adoption plan. In *agency-identified* adoption, the agency works with both prospective adoptive parents and birthparents who have contacted the agency seeking services. In an *agency-assisted adoption*, prospective adoptive parents work with their local agency, while using the services of another agency or facilitator (outside of Massachusetts) to locate a birthparent. In a *parent-identified adoption*, prospective adoptive parents identify a birthmother or birthparents through networking, and birth and adoptive parents agree to work together to make an adoption plan. A Massachusetts agency is used to coordinate the adoption process.

> *When you are participating in adoption, it is important to understand that the child—not the adults—is the primary client of the agency.*

When you are participating in an adoption, it is important to understand that the child — not the adults — is the primary client of the agency. The child is the most vulnerable person in the process and often, as in infant adoption, has no ability to participate in the decisions that will determine his or her future. In other words, the first consideration for any decisions that an agency makes must be based on the agency's assessment of the best interests of the child. This is required by standards of professional practice, regulation and law.

While many adoptive parents complete adoptions in which both the adoptive parents and the birthparents reside in the Commonwealth, there are also adoptions in which the adoptive parents reside in the Commonwealth and the birthparents live in another state where the infant is born. These are *interstate adoptions*. In these situations, Massachusetts agencies work closely with the agencies, attorneys and adoption professionals in other states to ensure that the procedures of both states are followed and that all appropriate legal issues are addressed and completed in the appropriate course.

Agency-Identified Adoption

In *agency-identified adoption*, you would be asked, after completing a homestudy, to put together materials to be used in the matching process with birthparents. These materials typically include a photo album, that provides a pictorial look at you, your home, interests and the way you live. Most agencies also use a "Dear Birthmother Letter," a personal communication to the birthmother. The photo album and letter introduce you to birthparents. Once these are complete, the matching process begins and most people are faced with some amount of waiting time.

Matching

The matching process, which brings adoptive parents and the birthparents who are considering adoption together, is an intense, emotional time. The match begins with "the call." Prospective parents receive a call from their agency telling them that a birthparent, who is either pregnant or has recently given birth, is interested in working with them. For some, this is the first time that the adoption of a child seems real. The matching and placement phases take different courses depending on the particular circumstances and preferences of the adoptive parents, the birthparents and the agency's procedures. Initial information that you can expect to receive at the time of the match will include the birthparents' first names and ages, the status of the child (if born) or pregnancy (including when the baby is due), any prenatal or background/descriptive information that is available at that time and any relevant legal information.

The process for matching often includes meetings and/or phone calls between adoptive and birthparents.

The process for matching often includes meetings and/or phone calls between adoptive and birthparents. While anticipation of the first contact can be exciting, it can also cause many worries for both sets of parents. The most common shared concerns are "Will they like us?" "What if we don't have anything to talk about?" and "Will they change their minds?" Fears and anxiety tend to melt away quickly as people get to know one another, talk about hopes for the child's future, and share feelings about the joys and worries of the adoption process. This is the beginning of a relationship between two families that, if the adoption proceeds, will always be a very important connection. In hindsight, most adoptive parents feel extremely fortunate to have had the opportunity to meet their child's birthparent(s).

Parent-Identified and Agency-Assisted Adoption

In an *agency-assisted adoption,* prospective adoptive parents work with their local agency while using the services of another agency, attorney or facilitator (outside of Massachusetts) to locate a birthparent. In a *parent-identified adoption,* prospective adoptive parents identify a birthmother or birthparents through networking, and birth and adoptive parents agree to work together to make an adoption plan. A Massachusetts agency is used to coordinate the adoption process.

Parents choosing either of these options may use the services of an attorney, out-of-state agency or adoption facilitator to network with birthparents.

Some people decide to locate birthparents themselves. They may network with friends and acquaintances and place out-of-state newspaper and other advertisements to identify birthparents interested in making an adoption plan. Advertising is regulated by each state and is prohibited in Massachusetts. Parents choosing either of these options may use the services of an attorney, out-of-state agency or adoption facilitator to network with birthparents. It is important to select an attorney, out-of-state agency or facilitator who is reputable and operating within the laws of his or her state. In both parent-identified and agency-assisted adoptions, it is likely that you will use the services of out-of-state agencies, adoption professionals, and/or attorneys to help manage the adoption process. Parents using these approaches should talk with Massachusetts agencies to clarify their procedures for working with in-state and out-of-state networking resources.

As with the agency-identified adoption, parents who use these approaches to domestic infant adoption will most likely need to compile a "Dear Birthmother" letter and/or pictures of themselves to be shared with potential birthparent matches.

Information About the Child

Massachusetts regulations require that adoptive parents receive information that includes, but is not limited to, "all information available regarding the medical history, mental health history, ... race and national origin of the child and birth family, and any other information which would be relevant to the growth and development of the child" and a "summary of the child's legal status" (see Resource Guide on page 72). While complete prenatal and birth records may not be available at the time of placement, the agency will be in close contact with medical staff to discuss the child's health status and any questions that arise.

Interstate Adoption

Whether an adoption is agency-identified, agency-assisted or parent-identified, when a baby is born out-of-state, the Interstate Compact for the Placement of Children (ICPC) regulates the movement of children across state lines. Each state maintains an ICPC office. ICPC administrators in both the "sending state" (the state in which the baby is born) and the "receiving state" (the state in which the adoptive parents reside) are required to review each adoption to ensure that proper legal procedures have been followed. No child can come to Massachusetts without the approval of the sending and the receiving states. While agencies and ICPC administrators work closely to complete interstate approval as soon as possible, it can take from several days to several weeks to complete the process.

Surrender or Termination of Parental Rights

Many individuals approaching the adoption process are concerned about the legal issues, especially the surrender of and termination of parental rights in a domestic infant adoption. In Massachusetts, birthparents cannot sign a voluntary surrender of parental rights until four days have elapsed from the date of the baby's birth. Each state has its own statues or regulations regarding when a surrender of parental rights may be signed and its revocability. Prospective parents, working toward a placement with birthparents from another state, should be sure to have their agency and/or attorney explain the requirements for their particular situation. Once a surrender of parental rights is signed, it is considered irrevocable. In situations where only one or neither birthparent has signed a voluntary surrender at the time a child is placed with the adoptive family, the placement is called a "legal risk placement."

In some situations, a birthfather may choose not to sign a surrender or the agency may have been unable to locate him. In these cases, agencies will follow the procedures for the termination of parental rights through the court system. This is most commonly referred to as the "210 petition." In this case, an attorney representing the agency will file a petition to terminate the rights of any named birthfather. Public notice must be given in the "legal section" of a newspaper. The location for such notice is determined by the court. This notice will run once a week for three consecutive weeks. If the birthfather does not respond by contacting the court, the agency may then return to court to have a termination order signed. In Massachusetts, an additional safeguard has been added to the termination procedure that terminates the rights of "all unknown and unnamed" birthfathers. This reduces the possibility of an unknown person coming forward at a later time to make claim to a child placed for adoption. To make use of this safeguard, agencies require a court termination process for most adoptions.

Parents should consult with their agency during the adoption process to determine the legal status of the birthparents and to ensure that they understand the plan for the termination of parental rights.

Parents should consult with their agency during the adoption process to determine the legal status of the birthparents and to ensure that they understand the plan for the surrender and/or termination of parental rights. Ideally, there should be a clear plan agreed upon by the agency, adoptive parents and birthparents. A plan doesn't guarantee that things won't change. In fact, agency professionals should talk to prospective adoptive parents about the likelihood of needing to adjust the plan, or the possibility that the birthparents may change their minds about placing their baby for adoption. Having a clear plan and understanding the risks will help you manage the experience successfully.

It is worth noting that adopting parents may choose to hire an attorney to provide consultation and representation during the adoption process, but it is the agency's attorney, not that of the adoptive parents (if they have one), who is typically responsible for processing the legal requirements of the adoption.

The Role of Attorneys

doption attorneys with significant experience and expertise in adoption law and practice may be useful to prospective adoptive parents. Their value depends largely on the type of adoption being pursued and what is happening in that process. Some prospective adoptive parents will find it useful to meet with an adoption attorney as a consultant to review their adoption options before deciding which type of adoption to pursue. Typically, an experienced adoption attorney will be familiar with the different types of adoption and the services available from Massachusetts and out-of-state resources.

Prospective adoptive parents often also consult adoption attorneys as they begin the actual adoption process. While review of agency paperwork may be useful, in a typical adoption a private lawyer will not be necessary to guide prospective adoptive parents through an uncontested adoption process, once they identify and select their local agency. One common exception may be in parent-identified or agency-assisted adoptions where frequently parents take a leading role in both locating the birthparent(s) and coordinating services for the birthparent, often in another state. Because of intricacies such as allowable expenses, birthfather rights, and interstate issues such as potential choice-of-laws or conflict-of-laws, and the Interstate Compact on the Placement of Children (the "ICPC"), a private attorney may provide invaluable assistance in ensuring as smooth a process as possible.

Private adoption attorneys may serve other functions as well. In a parent-identified adoption, they may be responsible for evaluating and retaining other professionals in situations where the birthparents live outside of Massachusetts, and coordinating the adoption process. In an agency adoption, a private attorney can be useful if specific questions or conflicts arise around issues such as allowable expenses, approaches to birthfather's rights, or negotiating an open adoption agreement in accordance with recently passed legislation.

In the rare event of a contested adoption, a private attorney may be the only way in which an adoptive parent can be assured of advocacy solely from their perspective. Keep in mind, however, that at least at the stage in which a birthparent's rights are being dispensed with (under G.L.c.210 Sec.3), the agency is typically the legal guardian of the child and the adoptive parent has no standing to be part of that proceeding. In addition, the agency's attorney is typically responsible for processing the legal requirements of the adoption. A good resource for contacting experienced private adoption attorneys is the American Academy of Adoption Attorneys (see Resource Guide on page 73).

An experienced adoption attorney will be familiar with the different types of adoption and the services available.

Birthparent Allowable Expenses

Infant adoptions from private agencies often include a fee for birthparent expenses. In Massachusetts, financial assistance for birthparents and associated fees that agencies may charge to adoptive parents are regulated by the state. In accordance with these regulations, agencies are permitted to provide payment to assist birthparents in obtaining adequate medical care, protecting their legal rights through legal consultation, providing transportation, obtaining medical services and legal counseling and other allowable services. Financial assistance may also be available to assist the birthmother with living expenses when her source of income or financial support is disrupted during her pregnancy. Agencies must complete financial assessments with the birthparents to determine their needs and the specific resources available to them.

Payments made to birthparents or service providers for any allowable expenses may be made only by the agency or other authorized persons. In some situations those may include attorneys and other professionals. It is illegal for prospective adoptive parents to make any payments directly to birthparents or to those who provide services to the birthparents. In situations where there are allowable expenses, adoptive parents may be charged for the cost of such expenses by the agency. When adoptive parents are charged for such costs, an itemized statement of expenses must be provided to them.

A Word About Birthparents

Birthparents care deeply about their children. Choosing adoption requires strength, courage and hard work.

In America, the media often portrays birthparents using negative, stereotyping images. Tragic situations are sensationalized, leaving the impression that all adoptions are at risk from birthparents. In fact, most adoptions are secure and successful. We rarely see stories that show positive images of birthparents or highlight successful adoption experiences for birth and adoptive parents. Unfortunately, this distorted representation leaves adoptive parents with an inaccurate image of birthparents. Birthparents, like adoptive parents, have a range of strengths and vulnerabilities.

Birthparents usually encounter difficult circumstances that lead them to decide that they are not able to provide for a child. These circumstances vary, but some birthparents feel they are too young to care for a child, while others feel their home environment is not safe or secure enough for a child. No matter what the situation, birthparents care deeply about their children which is why they are willing to choose a difficult and painful alternative. Choosing adoption requires strength, courage and hard work.

Having an informed image of birthparents, as well as developing understanding and compassion for your child's birthparents in particular, will make you a better parent through each stage of your child's development.

It can be particularly hard for someone seeking to adopt a child to empathize with someone who would consider placing a child for adoption. Learning about birthparents is an important part of becoming an adoptive parent. Having an informed image of birthparents, as well as developing understanding and compassion for your child's birthparents in particular, will make you a better parent through each stage of your child's development.

Adoption is fundamentally a cooperative process. Birthparents and adoptive parents are working together to make a successful adoption plan. Sometimes this work is directly connected when they meet and plan steps together and sometimes it is on parallel tracks. Adoptive parents and birthparents are not adversaries in the adoption process but rather are partners in this unique human experience.

Openness in Adoption

Openness refers to a spectrum of choices regarding information sharing and the amount of contact between the birth and adoptive families.

Practice in adoption is changing. It was historically common to see "closed" adoptions in which little or no information was shared between the birth and adoptive families with no contact between them. Over the last 30 years, we have learned that this closed approach to adoption has had many negative consequences for children, birthparents and adoptive families. Secrecy and a lack of information made it difficult for children to understand their characteristics, identity and why they were placed for adoption. It also put adoptive parents in the difficult position of not having access to information and understanding that could help them meet the needs of their child. The lack of information also posed problems for birthparents who would have benefitted from knowing about the well-being of their child. They would have been better able to resolve their grief and to have confidence in their decision to make the adoption placement. Increased "openness" in adoption has been a response to these and other issues.

"Openness" refers to a spectrum of choices regarding information sharing and the amount of contact between the birth and adoptive families. For many adoptive parents, this may mean meeting the birthparent(s) and sending periodic letters and pictures. This kind of openness is common in domestic infant adoptions and is often coordinated through the agency without disclosing identifying information such as last names and addresses. Other kinds of openness may include sharing identifying information and making plans to have contact during and after the adoption.

The degree of openness in an adoption depends on the individuals involved. Whatever form openness takes, it should be developed and managed with the best interests of the child in mind. Conversations with agency staff and other adoption professionals can help you and the birthparent(s) plan the kind of openness that fits for your adoption. Life is not static. Relationships take time to develop and openness plans can evolve as the needs of children and adults change. It is important to note that adoption, whether more "open" or more "closed,"

Adoption, whether more "open" or more "closed," creates a connection or relationship between the birth family and adoptive family that lasts a lifetime.

creates a connection or relationship between the birth family and adoptive family that lasts a lifetime.

One common fear among adopting parents when they first learn about openness is that contact with birthparents may pose a risk to the placement or that their roles as parents will be compromised. Virtually no evidence supports these fears. Birthparents do not make adoption plans for their children because they want to be co-parents. Birthparents tend to be very respectful of adoptive parents. It also appears that having some degree of openness serves as a reassurance for birthparents and actually enhances the security of the adoption.

3

International

Overview. 40
Two Basic Approaches 40
Health Concerns 41
Application Process 42
Immigration and Naturalization Service 42
Matching in International Adoption 44
Information About the Child 44
Processing the Adoption. 45
Adjusting to a New World. 46
International Adoption Documentation Checklist 46

Overview

Over the past decade, the number of international adoptions has increased dramatically. In 1998, American individuals and couples adopted 15,774 children from other countries. The U.S. Department of State reports that in 1998 nearly 1/3 of all international adopted children came from Eastern Europe, approximately 1/3 from China, and the remaining 1/3 from Central and Latin America, Africa, India and Southeast Asia.

If you are interested in international adoption, think about how comfortable you would be incorporating the ethnic and/or cultural heritage of a child born in another country into your family life. When you adopt a child from another country, you become a multicultural family. You can explore what this would mean by talking to friends, relatives and agencies, and reading and/or participating in programs that teach about families raising children from different ethnic and cultural heritages. Families who have adopted from other countries can be a great resource. They can provide information about the travel experience, conditions in the country and orphanages, and how their children are doing both in the short- and long-terms. Agencies and adoptive parent support groups can assist in putting pre-adoptive families in touch with other parents. The Internet provides another way to learn about recent adoption experiences and obtain up-to-date information (see Resource Guide, pages 70-74).

To complete an international adoption and bring a child to the United States, parents must meet the requirements of three systems. These include: the United States Immigration and Naturalization Service (INS), the foreign country in which the child resides, and the U.S. state in which the child and family will live. Regardless of the particular approach to international adoption, all prospective adoptive parents need to complete a homestudy and an INS form I-600A "Application for Advance Processing of an Orphan Petition," and apply for the child's immigration to the United States. Although these steps usually require much time and paperwork, they are intended to protect the interests of the child, birthparent(s) and adoptive parent(s) and to result in a secure adoption.

When you adopt a child from another country, you become a multicultural family.

Two Basic Approaches

There are two basic approaches to international adoption. You can use:

• Agencies in Massachusetts with international adoption programs in specific countries. These agencies coordinate all services needed for adoptions from those countries.

• Agencies that do not have internal international adoption programs. These agencies coordinate with other agencies, organizations or facilitators throughout the nation and abroad who have programs in specific countries. Massachusetts agencies that use this model will work with parents to complete the requirements for adoption in Massachusetts, while the other agency, organization or facilitator works with parents to identify a child and coordinate the services necessary to complete the adoption in the specific foreign country. In situations in which more than one agency or organization is involved, it is important to have a clear understanding of who is responsible for particular services.

It is important to investigate thoroughly the adoption procedures for a particular country and program before proceeding.

The procedures of international adoption incorporate the requirements of the Commonwealth of Massachusetts, the Department of State (through the Immigration and Naturalization Service), and the particular country. Procedures vary significantly from country to country, often influenced by the social, economic and political climate. As a result, there are variations, for example in the length of time involved, age requirements for parents and travel procedures. It is important to investigate thoroughly the adoption procedures for a particular country and program before proceeding. In addition to talking with agencies about programs in particular countries, you may also want to read the International Concerns Committee for Children (ICCC) Report on Foreign Adoption (see Bibliography page 75) and country alerts distributed by the Department of State (see Resource Guide page 74) for additional information.

Health Concerns

Children placed for adoption from other countries are in need of adoptive placement as a result of poverty, abandonment, the death or illness of their parent(s), or other family difficulties. Children may be cared for in orphanages and, while conditions in foreign orphanages vary greatly, overcrowding and limited resources (food, clothing, heat, water, medicine and toys) are realities many children experience. Prenatal and postnatal medical care is often limited as well. As a result, these children may be at risk for medical and developmental problems of which adoptive parents should be made aware. Adding to these issues are U.S. regulations (and sometimes foreign country requirements) stipulating that the child must have been abandoned to be eligible for adoption. This often means that there is little reliable information about the birth family or early life circumstances of the child. Conditions vary enormously from country to country and from orphanage to orphanage within a country. As you narrow your choices, try to speak with people who have first-hand knowledge and photographs of the specific orphanages or other facilities that will care for your child. Most agencies and parent organizations will be happy to connect you.

If you are considering international adoption, it is recommended that you consult with knowledgeable medical professionals who can help you understand the relevant health issues. Knowledgeable professionals can discuss medical issues relating to countries you may be considering as well as provide consultation about a particular child referred for placement. Agencies can usually provide you the names of such medical professionals. Other adoptive parents are also a good resource for referrals as well.

Application Process

If you are considering international adoption, it is recommended that you consult with knowledgeable medical professionals who can help you understand the relevant health issues (see Resource Guide page 71).

Families choosing to pursue international adoption must complete numerous forms, some of which may be repetitive. It is important to understand that the international adoption process means meeting the requirements of three entities: (a) the agency, which must meet the Massachusetts adoption regulations; (b) the Immigration and Naturalization Service (INS); and (c) the requirements of the country of origin of the child. The documents collected for the foreign country are commonly referred to as "the dossier." Your agency will advise you about the particular documentation needed for your adoption process.

The dossier for the foreign country will vary from country to country, but most countries will require, in addition to an approved homestudy, notarized copies of most of the documentation. Generally an *apostile seal* will be needed on notarized documents. Recognized by all governments, an apostile seal is a certification provided by the Massachusetts Secretary of State. These are available from the Secretary of State's Commissions Section, located on the 17th floor of the John McCormack Bldg., One Ashburton Place in Boston, (800-392-6090). The cost for the seal is $3.00 per notarized signature on your documents. In addition to these steps, most of these documents will be translated by an officially recognized translator.

Some foreign governments require the U.S. Department of State to authenticate documents in order for the documents to be considered legal. Primarily, these are countries that are not part of The Hague Convention on International Adoption. This process is called authentication and it is not the same as an apostile seal. The U.S. Department of State Authentications Office provides this service (see Resource Guide page 74).

Immigration and Naturalization Service

Prior to bringing an adopted child into the United States, the parent(s) must comply with the requirements of the Immigration and Naturalization Service (INS). A visa to bring an adopted child into this country will be issued only upon the determination of the INS that all requirements have been met. Your adoption agency will work closely with you to file all the documents needed by INS. It is important to follow carefully the instructions provided by INS to ensure the proper and timely processing of the documents.

A detailed presentation of INS requirements is available in INS publication M-249Y " The Immigration of Adopted and Prospective Adoptive Children." You can obtain these booklets and the telephone numbers of local INS offices in the United States by calling 800-755-0777. You can also get information on current forms, fees and fingerprinting procedures at the INS website (www.ins.usdoj.gov). The following information is an abbreviated outline of the forms and documents required for an international adoption.

Fees and processing times are subject to change.

- **INS form I-600A**, "Application for Advance Processing of an Orphan Petition," filed at the INS office in Boston. This is a general information form requiring that one of the applicants is a U.S. citizen, is at least 25 years of age, and includes proof of marriage (if applicable). A request should be made to forward this notice to the U.S. Embassy or consulate in the country of origin of the child. As of 1999, the fee for filing Form I-600A was $405. The processing time can take several months; placement agencies can provide the most accurate time estimate.

- **Approved homestudy, with supplemental documents and completed fingerprint form.** There is a $25 processing fee for fingerprinting.

- **Form I-864,** Affidavit of Support, which must be accompanied by certified copies of the tax returns for the three most recent years.

Upon approval of the I-600A, applicants and the agency will receive

- **Form I-71H**, "Notice of Favorable Determination Concerning Application for Advance Processing of an Orphan Petition."

After you have accepted the referral of a specific child for adoption and completed the adoption requirements of the foreign country, you will need to file INS form I-600. This "Petition to Classify an Orphan as an Immediate Relative" is filed after completion of the adoption requirements of the foreign country. The I-600 application will require specific information about the child including proof of the child's identity and proof of his or her orphan status. Also, proof that the adoption has been finalized through the foreign courts or that the court of authority has given the applicant guardianship of the child is necessary prior to the approval of the I-600 and the issuing of the child's visa. The process to accomplish this step is described in the next section.

Prior to issuing the child's visa, the U.S. Department of State also conducts the "I-604 Orphan Investigation." This investigation ensures that the child is an orphan as defined by U.S. regulations and that the child does not have any medical condition that the adoptive parents are unwilling to accept.

Matching in International Adoption

The typical matching process in international adoption, called the "referral," is different from that in domestic adoption. International agencies, agents, or facilitators get information from parents about the kind of child they are seeking to adopt. They also inform parents about the kind of children available through their particular program. Parents may be asked to complete a special needs questionnaire addressing physical and mental health issues that parents are or are not willing to accept. The information is used with the dossier by agencies, and the authorities in the foreign country, that make the decisions about which child will be matched with which parents.

Information About the Child

Once the referral is made, parents usually receive information about the child. This information may include pictures, videotapes, medical reports, reports on how the child came into care, experience in care and, if available, information about the birthparents. Reports may be in the language of that country and include terminology that, when translated, can be unclear and may not necessarily be accurate. In some situations, there may be little or no information about the birthparents. In addition, it may not be possible to verify what information is available.

Information about the child may include pictures, videotapes, medical reports, reports on how the child came into care, experience in care and, if available, information about the birthparents.

It is best to use agency personnel and medical and mental health professionals with specific knowledge of the country and, ideally, the orphanage or facility, to review reports with you to identify and address any concerns (see Resource Guide page 71). Talking to other parents who have completed international adoptions from the same country can also provide good perspective about the information you receive. When there are concerns, it is always worthwhile to ask the agency for more information. Sometimes it is possible to request and receive additional information or to arrange for additional medical evaluation.

After reviewing available information about the child and raising any questions and concerns, parents will need to decide if they can commit to adopt the child. The time frame for this decision varies from several days to several weeks. If you decide to go ahead with the referral, plans are made for travel and placement. Should you determine that you cannot go ahead with this particular referral, the agency or placement resource will want to understand the reasons for your decision to avoid repeating an unsuccessful process. Plans are then made to identify another child to refer.

Processing the Adoption

Most international adoptions are finalized (legally completed) in the foreign country. The legal process in some countries requires a waiting period between the filing of the legal documents (in the country's court system) and the actual court date for finalizing the adoption. Some countries require that the adopting parent(s) be present when the adoption papers are filed in the country's court, while others allow an attorney or other representative to complete this step. In most situations, the final adoption decree is completed prior to the State Department's granting a visa to allow the child to enter the United States.

In international adoption, at least one parent usually is required to travel to the specific country to complete the formal process and accept placement of the child.

In international adoption, at least one parent usually is required to travel to the specific country to complete the formal process and accept placement of the child. The procedures in the particular country determine the length of time that you would need to stay in that country and where you may need to travel within the country. Some agency programs organize groups of parents to travel together (with an escort), while others may send parents individually with escorts available when they arrive in the country. In some situations escort services may be provided to bring the child to the United States.

There is a value in travelling; you can experience the culture first hand. You can document your family story in pictures, words and artifacts that will help your child appreciate his or her early life. You will be able share more with your child about his or her heritage and how your family came to be.

To ensure the security of the adoption, families should consider re-finalizing their child's adoption through the Massachusetts courts.

To ensure the security of the adoption, families should consider re-finalizing their child's adoption through the Massachusetts courts. U.S. courts are not required to recognize a foreign court decree. As a result, a child's adoption status may be open to challenge. To complete this process, families work with their local agency to complete a post-placement process, in which the agency sends an adoption worker to meet regularly with the family between the time of placement and the time when the adoption can be re-finalized (minimum of six months). At the end of the post-placement process, the agency and its attorney will help the family, and frequently the family's attorney, file the required documents in the probate and family courts for the county in which the family resides. Probate courts in some counties have international adoption specialists who can provide you with helpful information on the post-placement process as well and can advise you on whether an agency is necessary.

A last step required in international adoption is to obtain U.S. citizenship for your child. To do this, it is necessary to complete a "naturalization" process. To begin the naturalization process, file INS Form N-643, "Application for Certificate of Citizenship on Behalf of an Adopted Child." As of 2000 the filing fee is $125. This process can take up to a full year.

Adjusting to a New World

Children coming to the United States from another country face a significant adjustment. They are leaving one world and entering an entirely new one. There are new people, smells, language, sounds, tastes, climate, foods and so on. Parents must help their children make this adjustment. Many agencies offer pre-adoptive educational programs for families adopting internationally to help parents prepare for this adjustment. Referrals for medical assistance and developmental support such as Early Intervention are available to help you meet your child's needs. Other adoptive parents or counseling services can help families to develop their own approach to learning about and respecting their child's heritage.

INTERNATIONAL ADOPTION DOCUMENTATION CHECKLIST

Some or all of the following items may be required by the adoption agency, attorney, U.S. embassy, INS or the state.

You can use the following checklist to help you organize your documents:

- ❏ Birth Certificate
- ❏ Child Abuse Clearance
- ❏ Divorce/Death Certificate
- ❏ Financial Statement
- ❏ Foreign Adoption/Custody Decree
- ❏ Foreign Birth Certificate for the Child
- ❏ Foreign Passport for the Child
- ❏ Homestudy
- ❏ Letters of Recommendation

- ❏ "Orphan" Status Document
- ❏ Photographs of the Family
- ❏ Photographs of the Child
- ❏ Physician's Report
- ❏ Physician's Report of the Child
- ❏ Police Certificate
- ❏ Power of Attorney
- ❏ Verification of Employment
- ❏ 1040 — Front Two Pages

Notes

4

Adopting a Waiting-Child

Overview 50
Placement of Siblings 52
Application 52
MAPP Training and Homestudy 52
The Match Process 53
Placement Planning 54
Post-Placement Process .54

Overview

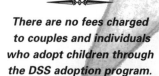

Throughout the country, more than 100,000 children need permanent, loving homes. These children are in the care and custody of state child welfare agencies as a result of abuse and/or neglect. In Massachusetts, the state child welfare agency is the Department of Social Services (DSS). In 2000, DSS is responsible for the well being of more than 10,000 children in foster care ranging from 0 to 18 years of age. More than 3,000 of these children have a case-plan that calls for permanent adoptive placement. DSS and private agencies that work with DSS have been successful in finding pre-adoptive homes for the majority of these children. However, in 2000 there are more than 800 children still in need of permanent families and each year additional children in the care of DSS become available for adoption.

To meet the needs of children waiting for permanent families, the DSS adoption program works with individuals and couples seeking to adopt children who are in the legal custody of DSS. There are no fees charged to couples and individuals who adopt children through the DSS adoption program. In addition, a number of private agencies have contracts to assist DSS in the placement of waiting children. Such agencies can coordinate the adoption process for people who are seeking to adopt a child in need of a family (see Resource Guide pages 77-80). Such private agencies may charge fees for their services, though many have indicated that they will waive or reduce fees for people who adopt waiting children (see page 59).

Many of the children available for adoption through DSS are considered children with "special needs." These are often children for whom traditional efforts to find families have not been successful. They may have physical or mental disabilities, medical, emotional and/or psychological problems. They may also be older, a part of a sibling group that needs to be placed together, or of a particular ethnic group. Children designated as having special needs due to these issues are eligible for an adoption subsidy (see page 60). Although the idea of special needs raises concerns, it is important to realize that there are many different kinds of special needs adoptions.

Some children from DSS do not fall into this "special needs" category, but may have a range of particular needs. These may include special educational, counseling or support needs. A child who has suffered from abuse or neglect as well as from disruption of his or her birthfamily and who has faced the fears of an uncertain future while in foster care may require a great deal of time, love and understanding from an adoptive parent and family. Parenting such children can be challenging, but the rewards are also great as a child learns to attach, trust, have self-confidence and love. An important quality that all of the children in the care of DSS share is their "most special need" for permanent families who can provide love, safety, security and support.

The first step in exploring the adoption of a waiting child is to call DSS at 800-KIDS-508 to request information.

There are no fees charged to couples and individuals who adopt children through the DSS adoption program.

You can learn about adopting a waiting child by talking to DSS and/or private agency social workers. It is also advisable to talk to parents who have adopted through DSS, to adoption professionals, organizations, and to read about the experience (see Resource Guide pages 70-74). As with all adoptions, you should discuss your interest in adopting a waiting child with close friends and family to explore the amount of acceptance and level of understanding available from your support system. As you educate yourself, you may also need to educate your support network. You can then decide if this kind of adoption is right for you.

Children most often enter the care and custody of DSS when they have been removed from their birthfamilies as a result of neglect, physical, emotional or sexual abuse, parental drug addiction or family disintegration. At the time of an adoption placement, a child may be legally free, which means that birthparents' legal rights have been terminated by the court or voluntarily surrendered. In situations where the birthparents' rights have not yet been terminated or surrendered, such pre-adoptive placements are called "legal risk" placements. In most cases, when the goal for a child in the care of DSS is adoption, DSS works to terminate the birthparent's parental rights through the court system. When possible, DSS will work to obtain a voluntary surrender of parental rights from birthparents.

In 1997, 1,191 and in 1998, 1,176 children in the custody of DSS were adopted. These are the highest number of adoptions ever completed by the Department. The children are from many ethnic backgrounds and all age groups:

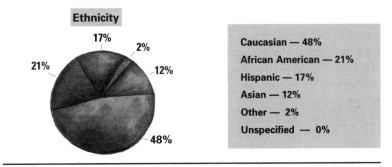

Ethnicity

17%
2%
21%
12%
48%

Caucasian — 48%
African American — 21%
Hispanic — 17%
Asian — 12%
Other — 2%
Unspecified — 0%

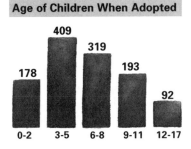

Age of Children When Adopted

178 | 409 | 319 | 193 | 92
0-2 | 3-5 | 6-8 | 9-11 | 12-17

1997 DSS data

Placement of Siblings

In 1997, DSS placed 265 sibling groups into permanent homes. Sibling relationships are important to all children and may be especially critical to children who have been removed from their parents. Whenever possible, efforts are made to place siblings together in adoptive families. In some situations, it is not possible to do this. In such circumstances, adoptive families may need to participate in sibling visitation plans. Visitation plans are developed as part of the placement plan and may involve foster and adoptive families, DSS caseworkers and other professionals.

Application

The basic requirement for adopting a waiting child is a safe and healthy environment. People over the age of 21 years can apply to become adoptive parents. They can be single or married, first-time or experienced parents. There are no minimum financial requirements for applicants, although it is required that your income is stable and that it can support the needs of a family. Home ownership is not required, but your living environment must meet basic safety and space requirements. To adopt a waiting child, the most important qualifications include an open heart, patience and resourcefulness.

To adopt a waiting-child, the most important qualifications include an open heart, patience and resourcefulness.

The first step in exploring the adoption of a waiting child is to call DSS at: 1-800-KIDS-508 to request information. (You can also contact private agencies listed at the back of this guide that make waiting-child placements). A DSS worker will answer questions you may have and, if you are ready to move forward, will complete an "Inquiry" form with you during this initial call. The worker will also mail a "Registration of Interest" form to you. Individuals interested in beginning the adoption process will be need to complete the form and a criminal background check application, known as the CORI form and return them to DSS. The working relationship with DSS begins with a home visit by an adoption worker. During this first visit, you will receive a full "Application" packet.

MAPP Training and Homestudy

Once the application is completed and received by DSS, applicants are invited to attend a multi-session training course, "Massachusetts Approach to Partnerships in Parenting" (MAPP). It is an important step in becoming a prepared and educated adoptive parent. MAPP training, led by a social worker and a foster/adoptive parent, provides pre-adoptive parents with a realistic view of the needs of children in the care of DSS. Through self-exploration, conversation with other parents, and learning from professionals, you can begin to develop tools that you will need to be a well-prepared adoptive parent. MAPP training is offered at DSS and at a number of private adoption agencies that work with DSS.

Upon the successful completion of MAPP training and additional home visits, the worker prepares the homestudy report that describes family history, strengths and limitations. DSS management staff review the homestudy report. Once the home study is approved, applicants are eligible for the placement of a child. Once you begin your MAPP training, the approval process generally takes 3 to 4 months. The time it takes to complete this process may be different if you work with one of the private agencies. After the approval, the wait for a match and placement begins.

MAPP training, led by a social worker and a foster/adoptive parent, provides pre-adoptive parents with a realistic view of the needs of children in the care of DSS.

While awaiting a match through the efforts of the area office or agency, there are additional resources that approved parents may use to learn more about children awaiting placement throughout the Commonwealth and the country. You can, for example, register with the Massachusetts Adoption Resource Exchange (MARE). MARE provides public service programs that can assist waiting parents to learn more about children in need of adoptive homes. You can review the MARE Manual, which provides information about specific children waiting for a home, at any public library or attend "matching" meetings. You can also review the Children Awaiting Parents (CAP) book, a national directory of photos and biographies featuring hundreds of children awaiting parents (see Resource Guide page 73). These are ways for you to work pro-actively toward your match. You can also use this waiting time to learn about post-placement resources, to read books on parenting and adoption, to attend adoption and parenting-related lectures, to join adoption and parenting support groups, and to talk with other parents who have adopted waiting children.

The Match Process

The match process is filled with both excitement and anxiety. During this process, approved families are presented with as much information as is known about a specific child. Information may include: the child's age and gender; race and ethnicity; current and past medical history; any mental health history (including psychological evaluations, developmental history, history of any physical and emotional traumas); education; special talents and interests; social history; placement history; and the birthfamily's medical and social histories. Information about the child's interactions with other children, adults, and caretakers, current living situation and his or her current legal status may also be included. At this stage, there is much for you to review and learn about the child you might adopt from written materials and from the adoption workers. In addition, depending on the circumstances and age of the child, this process may include conversations and meetings with the child and foster parents.

Placement Planning

The goal for the placement plan is to help the child make a successful transition from foster care to the adoptive home. The adoption worker assigned to the adoptive parents and to the child (or children) will work to support everyone throughout the process. The placement plan may include a series of short visits with the child in his or her foster home or in the home of the adoptive family as well as other planned activities with the adoptive parents. Often there is a progression to longer visits and overnight stays prior to the child moving to the adoptive home.

The placement plan may include visits with the child in his or her foster home or in the home of the adoptive family as well as other planned activities.

Children develop strong connections to their foster families and it may be in their interest to maintain contact with them. Foster parents can also be invaluable resources to help you learn about your child and help him or her to adjust to family life. The placement plan may include planned contact with the foster family over time. Many children, when placed for adoption, already have connections to counselors and medical professionals that may be important to maintain. Understanding the significance of these connections and making any plans for maintaining or transitioning them will be part of the work during this process.

Post-Placement Process

During this period, families may experience a roller coaster of feelings as they learn about and adjust to each other. Children — many of whom have been through several foster care placements — may feel unsure of what is expected of them, may be nervous about meeting new people and may doubt that they are truly in a permanent family. They may feel a sense of loss for their birth- and foster-parents and may try to test limits to see whether this will be their permanent home. Parents can experience a range of feelings including frustration, confusion, exhaustion and excitement. Flexibility and a willingness to ask for help are necessary to address the challenges that may arise during this adjustment period.

During this period, families may experience a roller coaster of feelings as they learn about and adjust to each other.

During this time, parents should expect, at a minimum, monthly visits from the adoption worker. Your adoption worker can assist you in understanding the adjustment process and the needs of your child. Connecting with and using the services of specialists may also be helpful to your newly expanded family. Your adoption worker can help you identify and work with medical and mental health professionals as well as special education programs that can provide services to help you meet the needs of your child. The process for finalizing an adoption of a waiting child is the same as that described on page 26.

Notes

5

Fees, Adoption Subsidy and the Adoption Tax Credit

Overview 58
Component Fees 58
Cost of Adopting 59
Costs in Waiting-Child Adoption 59
Financial Assistance 60
Adoption Subsidy 60
Adoption Tax Credit 61

Overview

Fees in the adoption process vary greatly.

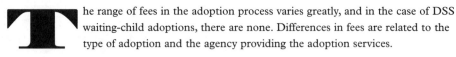

The range of fees in the adoption process varies greatly, and in the case of DSS waiting-child adoptions, there are none. Differences in fees are related to the type of adoption and the agency providing the adoption services.

Massachusetts adoption regulations require that agencies make some accommodation for individuals and couples who cannot afford an agency's standard fees. Some agencies offer sliding scale fee structures based on income.

Component Fees

Component fees that may be incurred in a domestic infant adoption include application, homestudy, placement, post-placement, legal, birthparent expenses and in the event of an interstate adoption, ICPC administrative fees. Out-of-state adoptions may also include fees for services provided by professionals in the other state. The chart below presents the typical component fees for infant adoption in Massachusetts.

Component Fees: Domestic Infant Adoption

Domestic Infant Adoption	Agency Identified Fee Ranges	Parent Identified or Agency Assisted Fee Ranges
Application	$0-$1000	$0-$500
Homestudy	$1,000-$3,400	$1,000-$3,400
Placement	$7,500-$29,000	$0-$14,000
Post-Placement	$800-$2,200	$800-$2,200
Legal	$650-$1,500	$0-$1,000
Birthparent Expenses*	$0-$7,500	$1,500-$7,000

Fees reported in Center for Adoption Research 1999 Massachusetts Agency Survey.
*Estimate based on national reports.

For international adoption, typical component fees include the application, homestudy, country specific fees, post-placement fees and legal fees. In addition to these fees, there are costs for the INS processing and document translation and authentication. The chart which follows presents the fees for international adoption services provided by Massachusetts' agencies.

Component Fees: International Adoption

International Adoption	International/ Agency's Program Fee Ranges	International/Networking With Other Programs Fee Ranges
Application	$0-$500	$0-$500
Homestudy	$850-$3,400	$100-$3,400
Placement	$1,000-$15,000	$0-$18,500
Post-Placement	$700-$1,800	$900-$10,500
Legal	$0-$220	$250-$850

Fees reported in Center for Adoption Research 1999 Massachusetts Agency Survey.

Massachusetts regulations require that agencies provide "fee information to prospective applicants in writing at the time of initial inquiry." In addition, agencies are required to provide an itemized statement of expenses prior to the placement of a child.

Cost of Adopting

Range

Domestic Infant/Agency's Resources	$4,000-$31,000
Domestic Infant/Parent Identified/Agency Assisted	$1,500-$12,000
Domestic Infant/Network with other programs	$600-$13,250
International/Agency's Programs	$3,000-$21,000
International/Networking with other programs/agents	$250-$20,000

Fees reported in Center for Adoption Research 1999 Massachusetts Agency Survey.

Costs in Waiting-Child Adoption

DSS does not charge fees for any part of their adoption process. Many private agencies reduce or waive fees for couples or individuals who adopt waiting children. In some situations when using a private agency, however, you may have to pay application and homestudy fees and possibly hire an attorney. There may also be other costs associated with waiting-child adoptions including medical, counseling and travel.

Financial Assistance

he costs of adoption can be substantial. There are several resources for financial assistance. These include:

- bank loans (some banks offer special loan rates for adoption expenses). There are also loans and grants available through the National Adoption Foundation, 800-448-7061;
- employer adoption benefits that may include reimbursement for costs, paid or unpaid time-off and other support services (National Adoption Center, 800-862-3678);
- tax credits and exclusions (see below);
- adoption subsidies (see below).

Adoption Subsidy

For additional information about adoption subsidies, call Department of Social Services State Subsidy Department at 617-748-2000 or 800-835-0838.

ederal and state subsidy programs, also referred to as "adoption assistance," are available to families adopting children with special needs to assist families in providing the necessary services and the financial resources to meet the child's ongoing needs. Adoption subsidy may be available to children adopted both through the Department of Social Services and private adoption agencies. For those adopting from private agencies however, it may be more difficult to have an application for subsidy approved. In either case, adoption subsidy is not designed to cover the full costs of adopting or supporting a child.

The Title IV-E Adoption Assistance Program, established by Congress in 1980, provides financial assistance to meet a range of needs for eligible children. While each state determines specific qualifications for children, the Federal Government mandates that children must meet the following requirements to receive a Title IV-E subsidy:

- The court has ordered that the child *cannot* or *should not* be returned home to the birthparent;
- The child is considered a "special needs child," as defined by each state; and
- The child could not be placed without a subsidy.
- In addition, prior to adoption, the child must have been eligible for assistance under Aid to Families with Dependent Children (AFDC) or Supplemental Security Income (SSI).
- Title IV-E Adoption assistance is based upon the needs of the child, not on the income of the adoptive parent.

The benefits available through the adoption subsidy program are determined on a case-by-case basis. Benefits may include monthly cash payments, medical assistance through Medicaid coverage and social services including counseling.

For additional information about adoption subsidies, call Department of Social Services State Subsidy Department at 617-748-2000 or 800-835-0838. Information is also available through the North American Council on Adoptable Children (NACAC) at 1-800-470-6665.

Adoption Tax Credit

Request IRS Publication 968 "Tax Benefits for Adoption" to learn more about tax credits.

To offset adoption expenses and to encourage adoption, Congress enacted a tax credit for qualified adoption expenses and a new exclusion for employer-provided adoption assistance programs. This credit is available to families who adopt privately or through the public system. Depending on your income, you may be eligible for a credit of up to $5,000 for certain expenses incurred in adopting an eligible child. The limit is $6,000 for adoption of a special needs child.

Appropriate expenses include reasonable and necessary adoption fees, court costs, attorney fees, travel and other direct expenses for the legal adoption of an eligible child. Expenses that are reimbursed by your employer or any government program are excluded from the credit. The adoption tax credit is due to expire on December 31, 2001, unless Congress re-authorizes it.

If you are interested in learning more about the adoption tax credit you can request IRS Publication 968 "Tax Benefits for Adoption." Information is also available on the web at *http://www.irs.ustreas.gov/prod/forms_pubs/pubs/p968toc.htm,* or by calling 800-829-3676.

6

After You Adopt

Finalization is a Beginning .64
Growing Up With Adoption 64
Many Kinds of Adoption .65
Post-Adoption Support and Services 66

Finalization is a Beginning

Families meet challenges best when they can make sense of them. Understanding how adoption affects children and families can help parents respond to their children's needs with sensitivity and perspective.

Adoption is a wonderful way to create or add to a family. It is also a different way. Adopted children, adoptive parents and their families deal with the differences as they experience each stage of development. In addition, depending on the approach taken in the adoption, a variety of issues may arise. Infant adoption, international adoption and waiting-child adoption bring together children and parents from vastly different life situations. While most adoptive families are healthy and raise their children successfully, certain predictable issues common to adoptive family life can pose special challenges.

Families meet challenges best when they can make sense of them. Understanding how adoption affects children and families can help parents respond to their children's needs with sensitivity and perspective. This section will describe some of the themes that are common to adoptive family experience, but may be different from non-adopted families.

Growing Up With Adoption

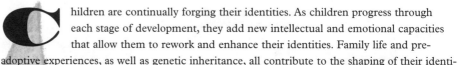

Children are continually forging their identities. As children progress through each stage of development, they add new intellectual and emotional capacities that allow them to rework and enhance their identities. Family life and pre-adoptive experiences, as well as genetic inheritance, all contribute to the shaping of their identities. For an adopted child, the process of identity development can be complicated. An adopted child has more than one heritage to integrate into his or her identity. Adoptive families often don't have the birthfamily information or stories to help reinforce aspects of basic identity. Without such information adopted children may face a greater challenge in creating an integrated and complete sense of identity .

An adopted child's self-concept is also highly influenced by his or her parents' attitudes and feelings about his or her birthparents. This makes it very important for adoptive parents to reach a level of understanding and comfort with the image and reality of birthparents and birth family, and their significance in the life of the child.

The experience of loss affects each member of the adoption triad. Just as adopted children have lost connection to their birth families, adoptive parents have often experienced the loss of a birth child they could not have. The birthparents have also experienced loss, as they have lost a connection to their biological child. Such losses have an important, though sometimes subtle, impact on individual and family development. How an adopted child experiences this loss may affect his or her sense of belonging and feeling whole, both in the family and in his or her life.

Fortunately, adoptive parents most often bring strength, wisdom and sensitivity to their families. These qualities help them meet the challenges of adoption.

Issues of identity and loss may affect each stage of family development. The impact of these issues can range from barely perceptible to intense. When issues do come up, they may reflect themes typical of a particular stage. For example, a fifth- or sixth-grader whose assignment is to trace his or her family tree. Adoptive families have to answer additional, complicated questions about where birthparents and birth family fit in their family tree. It also raises questions about what is private and the difference between privacy and secrecy. This can be very challenging. Adoptive parents may need to sensitize educators — teachers and counselors — to the ways in which adoption may come into play in school and other social experiences.

Adoption is an ongoing experience for children, but not always the most important one. Adoptive parents must be mindful of the impact of adoption, but also must recognize that not every concern that arises in their family is necessarily adoption-related. With education, support and communication, parents can develop their skills and be comfortable trusting their instincts. After all, parents are the true experts when it comes to their children.

Adoptive parents must be mindful of the impact of adoption, but also must recognize that not every concern that arises in their family is necessarily adoption-related.

Many Kinds of Adoption

Appreciating differences and learning about the unique needs and strengths of your child are essential, not just to adoptive parenting, but to all parenting.

Talking to your child, communicating with schools and others about adoption, and helping children make sense of adoption as they grow are some of the general challenges facing adoptive families today. For some families, understanding issues related to international, transracial, older child and special needs adoption are critical to their success and well-being. Appreciating differences and learning about the unique needs and strengths of your child are essential, not just to adoptive parenting, but to all parenting.

With adoption, parents must learn to differentiate among concerns that may be adoption related and those concerns that may be developmentally related, or reflect unique characteristics of their children. Issues like these require you to identify supportive resources that might help you address them. The resources described below and in the guide at the back of this book can provide some direction.

Post-Adoption Support and Services

Many agencies offer post-adoption resources. There are many support programs, independent counselors, educators and physicians who provide sensitive knowledgeable services for adoptive families. A good way to identify these professionals is by asking your agency. Other good resources for networking with families and accessing information and support programs are the Open Door Society (ODS) and Adoptive Families Together (AFT) (see Resource Guide pages 70 and 71).

In Massachusetts, there are two state-funded programs that provide post-adoptive services for families throughout the Commonwealth, KidsNet and Adoption Crossroads.

The Massachusetts Society for the Prevention of Cruelty to Children (MSPCC) KidsNet program offers extensive services for foster, kinship and adoptive parents connected with DSS. These services include child-care, respite, training, support groups, advocacy, membership services and community support. Services are offered through regional offices. To obtain information about regional KidsNet programs, contact the central administration at 617-587-1500 or visit the KidsNet Connection Website at *www.mspcc.org.*

Adoption Crossroads is a state funded post-adoption support service program open to all adoptive families. The program provides information and referral services, counseling, support groups and networks, respite services, mentor families and training. Services are available through regional centers. To obtain information about regional Adoption Crossroads services call 800-972-2734.

Notes

Resource Guide

Support and Informational Resources 70

Bibliography 74

Adoption Agencies 76

Support and Informational Resources

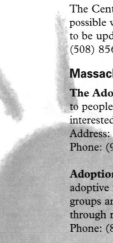

The Center for Adoption Research has attempted to include as many organizations as possible within this resource directory. If any of the resource information is incorrect or needs to be updated or if any organization was unintentionally missed, please contact the Center at (508) 856-5397.

Massachusetts Based Resources

The Adoption Connection provides assistance with search in adoption and provides support to people who were adopted, birthparents, and adoptive parents who are involved in or are interested in search issues.
Address: 11 Peabody Sq., Rm. 6, Peabody Square, Peabody, MA 01960.
Phone: (978) 532-1261.

Adoption Crossroads is a state funded post-adoption support service program open to all adoptive families. The program provides information and referral services, counseling, support groups and networks, respite services, mentor families and training. Services are available through regional centers.
Phone: (800) 972-2734.

Adoptive Families Together (AFT), is a supportive network of adoptive families who share experiences and information to strengthen our families and our adoptions. AFT believes that adoptive families are the true experts on the raising of adopted children, and brings families together in order to gather and disseminate information.
Address: 418 Commonwealth Avenue, Boston, MA. 02215-2801.
Phone: (617) 57-ADOPT.
Website: http://www.adoptivefamilies.org/aft/.

Families With Children From China New England (FCC)
• FCCNE/South Shore — Membership includes towns south of the City of Boston. For information, please contact Judy Collins at (781) 740-2997 or email: britsmum@aol.com.

• FCC Metrowest — To join call Rika Smith McNally at (508) 650-0374 or email: jmcnally@mit.edu.

• Nashoba FCC — For information contact Jane Mosier at (978) 897-3491 or email jmosier@modavi.com.
Website: http://www.fccne.org

Families with Khmer Kids
20 Oakhurst Ave., Ipswich, MA 01938.

Massachusetts Adoption Resource Exchange, Inc. (MARE), is a non-profit agency that provides adoption information and referrals to the general public.
Address: 45 Franklin St., 5th Floor, Boston, MA 02110-1301.
Phone: (800) 882-1176.
Website: http://www.mareinc.org.

Massachusetts Bar Association provides an attorney referral service.
Address: 20 West Street, Boston, MA 02111.
Phone: 617-338-0500.

The Massachusetts Society for the Prevention of Cruelty to Children (MSPCC)
KidsNet program offers extensive services for foster, kinship and adoptive parents connected
with DSS. These services include child-care, respite, training, support groups, advocacy, membership services and community support. Services are offered through regional offices. To
obtain information about regional KidsNet programs contact the central administration.
Phone: 617-587-1500.
Website: http://www.mspcc.org.

The Open Door Society of Massachusetts, Inc. (ODS), is a non-profit organization providing support and education to all people who have been touched by adoption. ODS head-
quarters are located in Holliston, Massachusetts. They also have numerous local chapters
throughout Massachusetts.
Phone: 508-429-4260 or 1-800-93 ADOPT.
E-mail: odsma@ma.ultranet.com.

Resolve of the Bay State, is the Massachusetts chapter of RESOLVE, a national, non-profit
organization providing individuals and couples with assistance in resolving their infertility
through education, advocacy and support.
Address: P.O. Box 541553, Waltham MA, 02454-1553.
Phone: 781-647-1614.
E-mail: resolvebaystate@erols.com.
Website: http://www.resolveofthebaystate.

Single Parents for the Adoption of Children Everywhere (SPACE), is a support and
information group for single people who have adopted or are interested in adopting, and the
children of those families.
Address: 6 Sunshine Ave., Natick, MA 01760.
Phone: 508-655-5426.
Email: maspace@aol.com.

Adoption Medical Resources
International Adoption Clinic
Children's Hospital
300 Longwood Avenue, Boston, MA 02115
Contact: Lisa Albers, M.D. Phone: 617-355-5209.

International Adoption Clinic
New England Medical Center
755 Washington Street, Boston, MA 02111
Contact: Laurie Miller, M.D. Phone: 617-636-8121, Website: www.nemc.org/adoption.

Pediatric Adoption and Foster Care Medical Services
UMass Memorial Healthcare
55 Lake Avenue North
Worcester, MA 01655
Contact for Domestic Adoption and Foster Care:
Linda Sagor, M.D., M.P.H. Phone: 508-856-4198.
Contact for International Adoption:
Richard Moriarty, M.D. Phone: 508-856-3947.

Massachusetts Licensing Authority

Office of Child Care Services (OCCS), is the licensing authority for Massachusetts' adoption agencies. OCCS provides lists of licensed adoption agencies, information about adoption regulations (Section 102 CMR 5.00: STANDARDS FOR THE LICENSURE OR APPROVAL OF AGENCIES OFFERING CHILD PLACEMENT AND ADOPTION SERVICES) and handles complaints against adoption agencies.
Address: One Ashburton Place, Boston, MA 02108.
Phone: 617-626-2000.
Website: http://www.qualitychildcare.org/.

National Resources

Adopted Child a monthly publication by Lois Melina, provides advice, insight and support to parents and professionals about the issues unique to parenting adopted children at all stages of family life.
Address: P.O. Box 9362, Moscow, ID 83843.
Phone: 1-888-882-1794.
Website: www.raisingadoptedchildren.com/news/index.html.

Adopting.com is an Internet resource index.
Website: www.adopting.com.

Adopting.org is an Internet resource and support organization.
Website: www.adopting.org.

AdoptINFO provides a collection of information, research, opinion and policy documents related to adoption and issues facing adoptive families.
Website: www.cyfc.umn.edu/Adoptinfo/.

Adoptive Families of America (AFA), is a private, non-profit membership organization of families and individuals providing information on and assistance with adoption.
Address: 2309 Como Avenue, St. Paul, MN 55108.
Phone: (612) 535-4829 or (800) 372-3300.
Website: http://www.adoptivefam.org.

American Academy of Adoption Attorneys (AAAA), is a national association of attorneys who practice in the field of adoption law. The Academy provides a nationwide directory of adoption attorneys, publishes a newsletter, holds annual meetings and educational seminars.
Address: P.O. Box 33053, Washington, DC 20033-0053.
Phone: (202) 832-2222.
Website: http://adoptionattorneys.org/.

Evan B. Donaldson Adoption Institute provides reliable information to enhance understanding and perception of adoption and inform policy and practice development. Excellent on-line bibliographic research database.
Address: 120 Wall St., 20th Floor, New York, NY 10005.
Phone: (212) 269-5080.
Website: www.adoptioninstitute.org/.

Families With Children From China (FCC), is a nondenominational organization of families who have adopted children from China. The purpose of FCC is to provide a network of support for families who've adopted in China and to provide information to prospective parents.
Address: 255 W. 90th Street-11C, New York, NY 10024.
Website: http://www.fwcc.org/.

Families for Russian and Ukrainian Adoption (FRUA), is a national network of parent support groups for families adopting from the former Soviet Union.
Address: P.O. Box 2944, Merrifield, VA 22116.
Phone: (703) 560-6184.
Website: http://www.frua.org.

Latin American Parents Association (LAPA), is a support network for parents who plan to adopt or have adopted children from Central and South America.
Address: P.O. Box 2013, Brick, NJ 08273.
Phone: (908) 249-5600.

The National Adoption Center — Faces of Adoption, is a non-profit organization whose mission is to expand adoption opportunities throughout the United States for children with special needs and those from minority cultures. The Center works with social workers and other adoption professionals to bring children and families together through a computerized photolisting of special needs **Children Awaiting Parents (CAP)** and adoption-related information on the Internet.
Address: 1500 Walnut Street, Suite 701, Philadelphia, PA 19102.
Phone: (215) 735-9988.
Website: http://www.adopt.org/.

The National Adoption Information Clearinghouse, (NAIC), is a federally funded resource service on all aspects of adoption, including infant, intercountry and special needs adoption.
Address: 330 C Street, SW, Washington, DC 20447.
Phone: (888) 251-0075.
Website: http://www.calib.com/naic/index.htm.

National Council for Single Adoptive Parents (formerly Committee for Single Adoptive Parents), is a support and information service that publishes a source book of domestic and intercountry adoption agencies willing to place with single applicants.
Address: P.O. Box 15084, Chevy Chase, MD 20825.
Website: http://www.adopting.org/ncsap.html.

North American Council on Adoptable Children (NACAC), is a nonprofit coalition of individuals and local adoptive parent support groups committed to meeting the needs of waiting-children and the families who adopt them. NACAC's activities include education, parent support, research and advocacy in the U.S. and Canada. They publish a wide range of material on foster care, older child adoption, transracial adoption, adoption subsidy and a quarterly newsletter, Adoptalk.
Address: 970 Raymond Avenue, Ste. 106, St. Paul, MN 55114-1149.
Phone: (651) 644-3036.
Website: http://members.aol.com/nacac.

Tapestry Books, The Adoption Book Catalog contains over 300 books on adoption and infertility for children and adults. Topics include how to adopt, learning about infertility, raising adopted children and more.
Address: P.O. Box 359, Ringoes, NJ 08551.
Phone: (800) 765-2367.
Website: http://www.tapestrybooks.com/.

The U.S. Centers for Disease Control (CDC), has information on suggested vaccinations and precautions for travelers.
Website: http://www.cdc.gov/travel/travel.html.

The U. S Department of State provides information about international adoption.
Website: http://travel.state.gov/children's_issues.html.

The U.S. Department of State Authentications Office provides authentication of documents for international adoption. Walk-in service is available 8 a.m. to 12 noon, Monday-Friday, except holidays. The Department charges $5.00 per document for this service, payable in the form of a check drawn on a U.S. bank or money order made payable to the Department of State. Documents mailed to the office for authentication require ten working days for processing.
Address: 518 23rd Street, NW, State Annex 1, Washington, DC 20520.
Phone: (202) 647-5002.

Bibliography

Introduction to Adoption

Bolles, Edmund Blair. (1993). *The Penguin Adoption Handbook*. New York: Penguin Books.

Gilman, Lois. (1992). *The Adoption Resource Book*. New York: HarperCollins.

Krementz, Jill. (1992). *How It Feels to Be Adopted.* New York: Alfred A. Knopf. Boys and girls from eight to sixteen years old share their feelings about adoption.

National Endowment for Financial Education. *How to Make Adoption an Affordable Option.* Denver, CO: National Endowment for Financial Education. This book provides information about expenses common to most adoptions, as well as those unique to the adoption of waiting-children, to independent adoptions, and to international adoptions. Addresses financial assistance and tax breaks available to adoptive parents. Available on-line at: www.nefe.org/adoption.

Nelson-Erichson, Jean & Erichson, Heino. (1993). *How to Adopt Internationally.* Los Ninos International Adoption Information Center.

Raising Adopted Children

Melina, Lois. (1986). *Raising Adopted Children.* New York: Harper Perennial. Guidebook that addresses experiences of adoptive parents and provides information about adoption's impact at different stages of child development.

Mintz, Margie. (1999). *Your Very Own Adoption Story.* Newton, MA: Conversations Press. This hands-on workbook provides an introduction to the adoption story for young children. It is most appropriate for domestic infant adoption experience. The book can be ordered on-line at www.margiemintz.com/adoptionbook.html or by calling 617-795-1654.

Turner, Carole S. (1999). *Adoption Journeys: Parents Tell Their Stories.* Ithaca, NY: McBooks Press. Adoption stories from different kinds of adoptive parents.

Van Gulden, Holly & Bartels-Rabb, Lisa M. (1994). *Real Parents, Real Children.* New York: Crossroad. Information about how adopted children think and feel about being adopted.

Watkins, Mary & Fisher, Susan. (1993). *Talking with Young Children about Adoption.* New Haven, CT: Yale University Press. Explores how children make sense of adoption, how it may appear in their play, and common concerns parents have. Includes accounts of conversations between parents and children.

International Adoption

Bascom, Barbara B., and McKelvey, Carole A. (1997). *The Complete Guide to Foreign Adoption: What to Expect and How to Prepare for Your New Child.* Ringoes, NJ: Tapestry Books.

Miller, Margi, and Ward, Nancy. (1996). *With Eyes Wide Open: A Workbook for Parents Adopting International Children Over Age One.* Ringoes, NJ: Tapestry Books.

Register, Cheri. (1990). *Are Those Kids Yours: American Families with Children Adopted from Other Countries.* New York: The Free Press. Information about children available for international adoption, how to adopt, children's adjustment and becoming an international family.

Report on Foreign Adoption (annual) includes information on health and development, INS requirements, post placement adjustment and development and agencies throughout the nation. Available through the International Concerns Committee for Children, 911 Cypress Drive, Boulder, CO 80303, Tel: 303-494-8333.

Transracial Adoption

Hopson, Darlene Powell & Hopson, Derek S. (1990). *Different and Wonderful: Raising Black Children in a Race-Conscious Society.* New York: Prentice Hall.

Gillespie, Peggy. (1999). *Of Many Colors: Portraits of Multiracial Families.* Ringoes, NJ: Tapestry Books. Stories of thirty-nine families who have bridged the racial divide through adoption or interracial marriage.

Pohl, Constance & Harris, Kathy. (1992). *Transracial Adoption: Children and Parents Speak.* New York: Franklin Watts.

Steinberg, Gail & Hall, Beth. (1999). *An Insider's Guide To Transracial Adoption.* Ringoes, NJ: Tapestry Books. Offers strategies for dealing with the challenges of multiracial family life.

Open Adoption

James L. Gritter, M.S.W., Editor. (1989). *Adoption Without Fear.* New York: Corona Publishing. Couples describe their experiences with open adoption.

Ruskai-Melina, Lois & Kaplan-Roszia, Sharon. (1993). *The Open Adoption Experience: A Complete Guide for Adoptive and Birth Families — From Making the Decision Through the Child's Growing Years.* New York: Harper Perennial. A guide to the issues and concerns of adoptive and birth families through the stages of open adoption relationships.

Severson, Randolph W. (1993). *A Letter to Parents ...On Open Adoption.* Garland, TX: Aries Center. Helpful information to prepare for an open adoption.

Adoption Agencies

The Public Agency

The Department of Social Services adoption program works with individuals and couples seeking to adopt children who are in their legal custody. For information about adoption call: 1-800-KIDS-508.

You can also contact the DSS regional offices:

- Boston Unit: 38 Wareham Street, Boston, MA 02118 (617) 574-8575
- Metro Unit: 30 Mystic Street, Arlington, MA 02474 (781) 641-8275
- Northeast Unit: 15 Union St., 2nd Floor, Lawrence, MA 01840 (978) 557-2500
- Southeast Unit: 141 Main Street, Brockton, MA 02301 (800) 432-6240
- Central Unit: 340 Main Street, Suite 570, Worcester, MA 01608 (508) 929-2150
- Western Unit: 1537 Main Street, Springfield, MA 01103 (413) 452-3350

Private Agencies

KEY TO TYPES OF ADOPTION	
AI: Agency Identified Domestic Infant. Agency is responsible for matching adoptive parents and birthparents. **PI:** Parent Identified Domestic Infant. Adoptive parents contact agency with an identified adoption plan. **AA:** Agency Assisted Domestic Infant. Adoptive parents and agency utilize the services of another agency to identify a match with birthparents.	**INT/AP:** International-Agency's Programs. **INT/N:** International-Network with other programs/agencies. **WC:** Waiting-Child Domestic. Adoption of children from foster care. Contracts with DSS to place children in adoptive families.

Act of Love Adoptions (MSPCC Subsidiary)
734 Massachusetts Avenue
Arlington, MA 02476
781-643-3443
Contact: Lisa Funaro and Ann Woodcock
Types of Adoption: AI

Adoption Resource Associates
124 Mt. Auburn Street
Cambridge, MA 02138
617-492-8888
Contact: Dr. Laura Nemeyer

Adoption Resource Center at Brightside
2112 Riverdale Street
West Springfield, MA 01089
413-788-7366
Contact: Jane Cohen
Types of Adoption: AI, PI, AA, INT/N

Adoption Resources
1340 Centre Street
Newton, MA 02459
617-332-2218
Contact: Jane Sullivan
Types of Adoption: AI, PI, AA, INT/AP, INT/N

Adoptions With Love, Inc.
188 Needham Street
Newton, MA 02464
617-964-4357
Contact: Nancy Rosenhaus
Types of Adoption: AI

Alliance for Children, Inc.
40 Williams Street
Wellesley, MA 02481-3902
781-431-7148
Contact: Vivian Cone
Types of Adoption: AI, PI, AA, INT/AP, INT/N

Beacon Adoption Center
66 Lake Buel Road
Great Barrington, MA 01230
413-528-2749
Contact: Deborah McCurdy, LICSW
Types of Adoption: WC, INT/N

Bethany Christian Services of New England
1538 Turnpike Street
North Andover, MA 01845
978-794-9800
Contact: Barbara G. Haynes
Types of Adoption: AI, PI, AA, INT/AP, INT/N

Boston Adoption Bureau, Inc.
14 Beacon Street
Boston, MA 02108
617-227-6308
Contact: Marilyn Speiser, LICSW
Types of Adoption: AI, PI, AA

Cambridge Adoption and Counseling
P.O. Box 425029
Cambridge, MA 02142
617-923-0370
Contact: Madeleine Daniels, LICSW

Cambridge Family & Children's Service
929 Massachusetts Avenue
Cambridge, MA 02139
617-870-4210
Contact: Alexis Silver
Types of Adoption: AA, WC, INT/N

Catholic Charities of Greater Boston
35 Bird Street
Dorchester, MA 02125
617-287-1150
Contact: Shirley Conway, LICSW
Types of Adoption: AI, PI, AA, INT/N, WC

Catholic Charities of Merrimack Valley
434 N. Canal Street
Lawrence, MA 01840
978-685-5930
Contact: Chris O'Shea
Types of Adoption: WC

Catholic Charities, Brockton
686 North Main Street
Brockton, MA 02401
508-587-0815
Contact: Susan Sullivan
All placements done by Catholic Charities of Greater Boston.

Catholic Charities, Diocese of Worcester
10 Hammond Street
Worcester, MA 01610
508-798-0191
Contact: Sara Glen

Catholic Social Services of Fall River, Inc.
783 Slade Street
Fall River, MA 02724-2509
508-674-4681
Contact: Mary-Lou Mancini
Types of Adoption: AI, PI, AA, WC, INT/N

Children's Aid and Family Service
Hampshire Co.
8 Trumbull Road
Northampton, MA 01060
413-584-5690
Contact: Priscilla Deane
Types of Adoption: AI, PI, AA, WC

Children's Friend, Inc., Hope Adoption
21 Cedar Street
Worcester, MA 01609
508-752-1456
Contact: Mary Maloney, LICSW
Types of Adoption: AI, PI, AA, WC

Children's Services of Roxbury, Inc.
2406 Washington Street
Boston, MA 02119-1733
617-445-6655
Contact: Valerie Lamar
Types of Adoption: WC

China Adoption With Love, Inc.
251 Harvard Street, #17
Brookline, MA 02446
617-731-0798
Contact: Lillian Y. Zhang
Types of Adoption: INT/AP

Concord Family Service
111 ORNAC
Concord, MA 01742
978-369-4909
Contact: Hope Rubin
Types of Adoption: AI, PI, AA, WC, INT/N

DARE Family Services, Inc.
17 Poplar Street
Roslindale, MA 02131
617-469-2311
Contact: Sheila Fitzgerald
Types of Adoption: WC

Downey Side, Inc.
999 Liberty Street
Springfield, MA 01104
413-781-2123
Contact: Mary Farrell
Types of Adoption: WC

Florence Crittendon League of Lowell, Inc.
119 Hall Street
Lowell, MA 01854
978-452-9671
Contact: Ilse Keegan
Types of Adoption: AA, INT/AP, INT/N

Full Circle Adoption Services and Family Building
39 Main St.
Northampton, MA 01060
413-587-0007
Contact: Marla Allison, JD, LICSW
Types of Adoption: AI, PI, AA, INT/N

Gift of Life Adoption Services, Inc.
1087 Newman Avenue
Seekonk, MA 02771
508-761-5661
Contact: Donna L. Ricci
Types of Adoption: INT/AP

Home for Little Wanderers
68 Fargo Street
Boston, MA 02210
617-428-0440
Contact: Paula Wisnewski
Types of Adoption: AI, PI, AA, WC, INT/N

Jewish Family Service of Greater Springfield
15 Lenox Street
Springfield, MA 01108
413-737-2601
Contact: Chaia Wolf
Types of Adoption: AI, PI, AA, INT/N

Jewish Family Service of Metrowest
475 Franklin Street
Framingham, MA 01702
800-872-5232
Contact: Dale Eldridge
Types of Adoption: AI, PI, AA, INT/N

Jewish Family Service of the North Shore
166 Essex Street
Salem, MA 01970
978-741-7878
Contact: Gloria Lippman-Barbacoff
Types of Adoption: AI, PI, AA, INT/N

Jewish Family Service of Worcester, Inc.
646 Salisbury Street
Worcester, MA 01609
508-755-3101
Contact: Stephen Slaten, Ph.D.
Types of Adoption: AI, PI, AA, INT/N

Love the Children of Massachusetts
2 Perry Drive
Duxbury, MA 02332
781-934-0063
Contact: Jean McNirnl
Types of Adoption: INT/AP, INT/N

Lutheran Social Services
of Massachusetts

416 Belmont Street
Worcester, MA 01604
508-791-4488
Contact: Sue Uryasz
Types of Adoption: AI, PI, AA, WC, INT/AP

MAPS International

400 Commonwealth Avenue
Boston, MA 02215
617-267-2222
Contact: Stephanie Mitchell
Types of Adoption: AI, PI, AA, WC, INT/AP

New Bedford Child
and Family Services

602 Purchase Street
New Bedford, MA 02740
508-990-0894
Contact: Ann Sanpeio
Types of Adoption: AI, PI, AA, WC

Protestant Social Services
Bureau, Inc.

776 Hancock Street
Quincy, MA 02170-9617
617-773-6203
Contact: Maryann Walsh
Types of Adoption: PI, AA, WC, INT/N

Wide Horizons for Children

38 Edge Hill Road
Waltham, MA 02451
781-894-5330
Contact: Jennifer Brown
Types of Adoption: AI, PI, AA, INT/AP

Notes

Notes

Notes

Notes